NATIONAL GEOGRAPHIC

THE

GREEKS

NATIONAL GEOGRAPHIC

THE
GREEKS

AN ILLUSTRATED HISTORY

DIANE HARRIS CLINE

NATIONAL GEOGRAPHIC

WASHINGTON, D.C.

CONTENTS

INTRODUCTION · · · · · · · · · · · · · · · · 6

MAP: OVERVIEW OF ANCIENT GREECE · · · ·8

CHAPTER I: DAWN OF THE GREEKS

    6000–1177 B.C. · · · · · · · · · · · · · 10

CHAPTER II: RISE OF THE GREEKS

    1177–508 B.C. · · · · · · · · · · · · · 76

CHAPTER III: BRIGHT, SHINING MOMENT

    508–323 B.C. · · · · · · · · · · · · · 122

CONCLUSION · · · · · · · · · · · · · · · 212

ACKNOWLEDGMENTS · · · · · · · · · · 215

FURTHER READING · · · · · · · · · · · 216

ILLUSTRATIONS CREDITS · · · · · · · · 218

INDEX · · · · · · · · · · · · · · · · 220

INTRODUCTION

THIS IS THE STORY OF THE ANCIENT GREEKS, whose legacy remains the foundation of Western civilization. From their emergence from the caves in 6000 B.C. to the death of Alexander the Great in 323 B.C., this book explains how the Greeks became the most enlightened civilization in the ancient world, and how archaeology and new scientific techniques are still revealing previously unknown aspects of their culture.

In Chapter I, we see how trade among the Cycladic islands developed around 2200 B.C., enriching all. By 1800 B.C., the Minoans were painting exuberant murals in their enormous palaces on Crete. By 1450 B.C., their island was occupied by the powerful mainlanders we call the Mycenaeans, who later Greeks remembered as the heroes who fought at Troy.

A cascade of shocks brought down the palaces around 1177 B.C., and Greece fell into a dark age. In Chapter II, we look at the Iron Age and the Archaic period. People retreated into the hills and were isolated for centuries. But they found comfort in stories, developing the myths that still echo through Western literature. By 800 B.C., villages expanded into urban centers. As people traded ideas, they became more adventurous, insatiably curious, and inventive.

In Chapter III, we explore the creativity of the classical Greeks, the civilization that developed philosophy, democracy, and more. Their poems, histories, epics, speeches, tragedies, and comedies preserve their ideals and values. The ancient Greeks left messages for us carved in stone and buried in earth. Their greatest hope was to be remembered.

ZAKYNTHOS: Boats on the island's coastline. "LADIES IN BLUE" FRESCO: *(page 2)* Minoan wall painting from Knossos. TEMPLE OF POSEIDON: *(previous pages)* Poseidon's temple at Cape Sounion, near Athens.

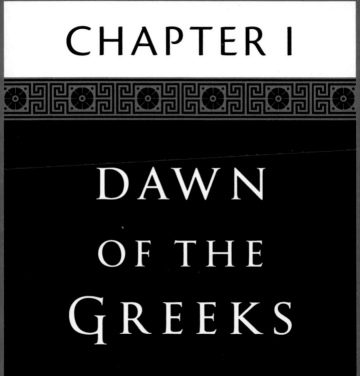

CHAPTER I

DAWN OF THE GREEKS

6000 B.C.

End of Neolithic period;
ancestors of ancient Greeks
start to practice agriculture

3000 B.C.

Early Bronze Age begins; rise
of Cycladic culture

2200 B.C.

Peak of Cycladic culture

2000 B.C.

Middle Bronze Age begins;
stone architecture,
fine ceramics

1800 B.C.

Minoans build palaces on
Crete, Santorini; earliest writing

1627 B.C.

Volcanic eruption on Santorini;
Late Bronze Age begins

1550 B.C.

Shaft graves at Mycenae;
begin writing Linear B

1450 B.C.

Mycenaeans take over
Crete; peak of trade and
interconnections with
Near East and Egypt

1250 B.C.

Trojan War

1177 B.C.

Attacks by Sea Peoples; collapse
of Bronze Age civilizations

THE FIRST GREEKS
6000–1177 B.C.

T HE REMARKABLE STORY OF THE ANCIENT GREEKS begins in the Franchthi cave, where humans lived from 38,000 to 3000 B.C. Located 60 miles south of the Corinth Canal, it provided shelter for nomadic Stone Age cave people, until they began to settle down and start farming. About a 4.5-hour drive south, another cave, Alepotrypa, was inhabited in the Neolithic era between 6000 and 3200 B.C. There, archaeologists uncovered the bones of at least 170 people. The cave was sealed in 3000 B.C. when a landslide blocked the entrance, leaving the bones undisturbed until recently. Some burials seem to be family groups, and one young couple were found cuddling, or as the archaeologist said in a 2015 interview, "They're totally spooning. The boy is the big spoon, and the girl is the little spoon: Their arms are draped over each other, their legs are intertwined. It's unmistakable." Life was tough; 31 percent died from blunt force trauma, and the average life span was just 29 years. A little tenderness made life and death bearable.

Small farming villages appeared in Greece in 3000 B.C., with domesticated animals and agriculture. People fished and hunted, but mainly ate what they grew. From such modest beginnings we will trace the development of Greek civilization, beginning with the Cycladic islands around 2200 B.C.

PRINCE OF THE LILIES FRESCO, KNOSSOS: *(opposite)*
Young man with elaborate headdress leads a procession.
MAP: *(right)* Modern Greece.

SHIPS, SEAFARING, AND SHIPWRECKS

GREEK HEROES ARE DIFFERENT from modern ones—they're more like the rest of us. They often fail, they are often punished or threatened by divine forces, and they suffer as often as succeed. In *The Odyssey,* Book 5, the hero, Odysseus, reaches his lowest point. On the sea, caught in a storm that Poseidon sent to punish him, Odysseus is blown overboard, and gasping for breath, makes it back to the surface and clambers onto his overturned ship, only to find that all his comrades were lost. As Odysseus learned, life was often risky, sometimes rewarding, and always challenged a person to give everything his spirit could muster to survive and succeed. External forces could bring unexpected surprises and obstacles, and it was the way in which a person dealt with them that made him a hero.

It should come as no surprise that, from earliest inhabitation, the culture of the people living in the area we now call Greece was tied to the sea, with the longest coastline of any country in the Mediterranean and 6,000 islands. Since the fifth millennium B.C., people have lived on the islands that form a circular shape in the middle of the Aegean Sea, called the Cyclades, or Cycladic islands.

All that we know about this earliest civilization in Greece in the Cycladic islands comes from archaeological evidence. We have no writing. But from the artifacts left behind, it seems that the residents of this circle of islands developed a collective culture that shared tastes and traditions.

By 3000 B.C., people began to make bronze tools by combining tin and copper, marking the beginning of the Bronze Age, which would last for the next 2,000 years. The copper has some local sources—closer in, Kythnos, and farther away, Cyprus—but the tin may have come from the area around Troy in northwest Turkey. The toolmakers must have had some trade and contact with people who could provide that tin.

In the Cycladic islands, the first users of bronze built settlements and sanctuaries. They buried their dead uncremated, placing them in a grave in contracted positions, accompanied by a few items including blades, ceramics, and figurines. Bronze artifacts found in the burials were mainly flat axes, chisels, tweezers, and needles.

These people traded goods between the various islands, including obsidian, which comes exclusively from Melos. Obsidian is a type of volcanic glass that is so sharp that surgeons still use it today; it was obviously prized in antiquity as well, for obsidian blades are found throughout the Cyclades. The people who quarried the obsidian built their houses right on the sea, and had no fortification walls. They were not afraid of outsiders.

From what we can discern, the Cycladic people of the Early Bronze Age sailed around among the islands, and lived off what they could catch, make, or grow. Farmers on these islands cultivated grapevines and olive trees, providing wine and olive oil. The Aegean is a bountiful sea, and seafood is still plentiful. Octopus and squid are local delicacies in the islands and coastal areas today, prepared with olive oil and salt over a grill. One senses that this is a very old recipe.

FRESCO, SANTORINI: Life in the Aegean centered on maritime activity. Marine Festival Fresco, 1650 B.C.

ANCIENT MARINERS AND THEIR NETWORKS

T HE PEOPLE OF THE AEGEAN COAST and island villages traveled and traded with each other via their busy network of shipping lanes. Ships and sailing technologies would be shared along such routes, but other sorts of networks piggybacked on these, such as food networks, trade networks, news and communication networks, and social networks. As is still the case today, frequent visitors to ports would become known to the locals, and relationships would be strengthened from island to island.

The mariners of the Cycladic islands cooperated with each other, working in teams on their ships. These were double-oared galleys, requiring more than one family to collaborate to fish or sail for trade. As would be the case in later classical cities, when men worked together on a ship, beating their oars against the sea in time to a coxswain's voice or pipe, it promoted harmonious relations and a sense of accomplishing something greater than themselves. The Greek way of life was social, political, and communal, and we see this trait in the Cycladic culture of the Early Bronze Age.

The islands each had their specialties. Naxos, the largest island, was known for its marble sources and forests; Siphnos for its mining of silver and lead; Melos for its obsidian. Interdependencies developed with these specializations, which encouraged cooperation among the islands. Population sizes ranged from communities with just a few dozen people to 1,000 or more.

Perhaps the cooperative spirit was partly due to their wanderlust; something about travel opens up the mind. To go out and return, a person must use skills and ingenuity to find ways around obstacles. Travel sometimes provides opportunities to experience freedom from self-restraint, and at other times makes one cling more closely to one's own traditions. Travelers to Greece today tend to visit the better-developed islands such as Santorini, Mykonos, Naxos, and Paros. But many of the smaller Aegean islands still retain their traditional ways and appearances. Whitewashed homes

SHIP MODEL, CRETE: Clay ship with raised bow and cylindrical spur, from Palaikastro. Early Minoan, third millennium B.C.

DOLPHIN FRESCO, KNOSSOS:
A view under the sea from above

with bright blue shutters are reached by narrow stone paths, surrounded by wildflowers and the sound of bells hanging from the necks of sheep. Mules with wicker baskets carry the day's supplies; neighbors stop to talk, tell stories, and wish each other well. Men sit in cafés, playing backgammon, smoking, and talking politics.

Village life 4,000 years ago is invisible in the archaeological record. We might find the foundations of the ancient café, a paving stone, a toy, a game piece, and many objects we cannot identify; without context, their function can be mystifying. We must reimagine the ancient world from its remaining fragments. Retracing steps on narrow paths, visitors can discover the continuity from the deep past to the present.

Island life fostered a cooperative mentality. Living on a rock in the sea, everyone was interdependent. The Greek people were travelers from these earliest times on throughout their history, sailing first in the Aegean Sea, then the Mediterranean and Black Seas. Sailing means risking it all. Those who sail believe the risk is worth the reward; they believe in themselves, they believe that they can outrun storms, outwit pirates, and outlast travails and hardships. The ancient Greeks were optimistic risktakers, leaning in toward the future on the boundless sea.

GREEK ISLAND LIVING

THE PEOPLE WHO LIVED ON THE CYCLADIC ISLANDS shared the same material culture, using the same kind of pottery for eating, drinking, and cooking; consuming the same diet; carving similar marble figurines, probably used for the same ritual purposes; and so on. This tells us that they sailed back and forth, trading material goods, swapping stories, and probably intermarrying.

Their modest homes, made of unworked fieldstones with mortar, were also built in the same style using the same techniques, regardless of the island. They must have liked having neighbors or family members nearby; their houses were built very close together with rectilinear floor plans. The floors were of earth or stone. Mats or rugs may have covered them, but they disintegrated long ago. These early builders made their roofs by laying branches on top of wooden beams, then packing earth over them.

CYCLADIC MARBLE FIGURINE

One set of artifacts left on the Cycladic islands by these Early Bronze Age people is both dazzling and puzzling. When we look at these 4,200-year-old figures, they look contemporary, like Picasso or Modigliani made them. These abstract white marble human figures, mostly nude females, are found in graves, settlements, and sanctuaries. They used to be called "Cycladic idols," but that implies they had a religious function, which they may not have. They range in height from three inches to four feet tall, carved from local marble sources in the islands. Some, if not all, were painted with mineral-based pigments, which would give color to the bright white marble figurines that we see now. Some are violin-shaped, with small heads, long necks, and round or triangular bodies, legless. Others look much more lifelike.

The women stand with slightly bent knees, their arms crossed over their swollen bellies, heads thrown back to face the sun. Sculpted curves emphasize the childbearing hips, rounded thighs, accentuated by a deeply carved groove between the legs. We would like to definitively say that these are fertility figures, but we only do this with a lack of certainty. They are so numerous that all we can safely say is that many Cycladic people owned them, handled them, traveled with them, left them at sacred spaces, and ultimately carried them to the grave.

CYCLADIC ISLANDS, MYKONOS: Traditional architecture on narrow streets resembles ancient town plans.

A few rare figures stand out: a man playing a double flute or panpipes; a lyre player seated on a chair, his head tilted back perhaps in ecstasy, or in song. We would have no knowledge of these musical instruments without these figures. The flute and the lyre are the most popular instruments in classical times as well, some 1,500 years later. This is proof that music and song have always been a part of Greece and its people.

Around 2000 B.C. something begins to happen on Crete, the large island south of the Cyclades. What makes this different from the Cycladic culture that came before is the presence of larger buildings, which were called palaces, or court compounds as some prefer to call them. They are really just an agglomeration of rooms without regard to symmetry. Whereas the Cycladic people wanted to live in independent houses, these people lived in basically a housing project. Five places on Crete have been found that share this same architecture between 2000 and 1700 B.C. The protopalatial architecture is the origin of the grand Minoan palaces we look at next, with central courtyards and more than 1,000 rooms. The Egyptians shared their technology for building with quarried stone.

MARBLE LYRE PLAYER, KEROS:
This seated musician entertains us still.

THE MYSTERY OF THE FRYING PANS

MADE OF CLAY, often incised with scenes of ships on the sea, pan-shaped objects with two-forked handles dating to around 2000 B.C. have been found on many Cycladic islands. We still don't understand what these curious instruments were used for. Many have spirals covering most of the surface, usually interpreted as water or waves, some with multi-oared ships in the midst of them. Toward the handle, a triangle that bears resemblance to a woman's anatomy is usually scratched into the clay. They are called frying pans because of their shape, but there are no fire marks. On the back side is a shallow rim that lifts the object off the table by an inch or so, when it is lying flat. Cycladic frying pans have been found in settlements as well as graves, so any religious function would need explanation. They might have been mirrors, if filled with dark olive oil. Maybe they are just plates, with handy rims to keep food from spilling while dining picnic style on the floor. It's a mystery.

FRYING
PAN

THE MINOAN PALACES ON CRETE IN THE MIDDLE BRONZE AGE

T HE PALACES ON CRETE are engineering marvels, elegant in form and painted with brightly colored frescoes—plaster that's painted when it's wet—over their handsome stone walls. Staircases provided stadium seating facing the large courts; smaller wings also have light wells and small courts to provide light and circulate air. Windows in the living areas may have been filled in with thin sheets of alabaster, a translucent stone to let in light and block the wind. The buildings had stone pavements, and running water piped in from natural springs. Toilets flushed through buried sewers. Large clay bathtubs provided a way to relax at the end of a day; fires in small hearths made spaces cozy.

When the British archaeologist Sir Arthur Evans discovered the first of these ancient complexes on Crete at the turn of the 20th century, he called it a "palace" after the grand structures he knew from England. Although "palace" probably wasn't the best word—because it suggests royalty and a rigidly hierarchical society with more command and control than was likely the case—the term stuck, due partly to Evans's discovery of a throne room.

FRESCO, KNOSSOS: Stylish female dubbed "La Parisienne," discovered in 1901

The stone chair that he identified as a throne is attached to the wall, with painted griffins (half panther, half bird) flanking both sides. The room is predominantly painted crimson, feeling quite grand and regal. A large stone bowl in the center may have been used for ritual libations. Up to 30 people could sit on the benches attached to the walls, which may indicate that a council met there. Petitioners entered the room after passing a gantlet of narrow hallways, perhaps manned by sentries.

We know nothing about the person seated on the throne at the Palace of Knossos. Male or female, young or old, priestly or worldly—we

SIR ARTHUR EVANS

THE PALACE AT KNOSSOS and the other palaces on Crete are large complexes, three and four stories high with at least one central open court. The largest holds about 1,400 rooms for living, manufacturing, storing, and record keeping. Evans called the people of the Middle Bronze Age on Crete "the Minoans," after the legend of King Minos who ruled Crete. According to the story, his wife, Pasiphae, mated with a bull and gave birth to the dangerous Minotaur. They kept him in a labyrinth where he ultimately was slain by the Athenian hero Theseus.

Evans was attracted to the site because, as a curator at the Ashmolean Museum in Oxford, he had come across a few Bronze Age artifacts with peculiar lettering on them. All were said to have been discovered on Crete. In 1900, having bought the land around Knossos, he began an excavation. Between 1900 and 1905, astonishing finds came to light, including some 3,000 clay tablets with the writing that so intrigued him, which he called Linear A. It remains undeciphered to this day.

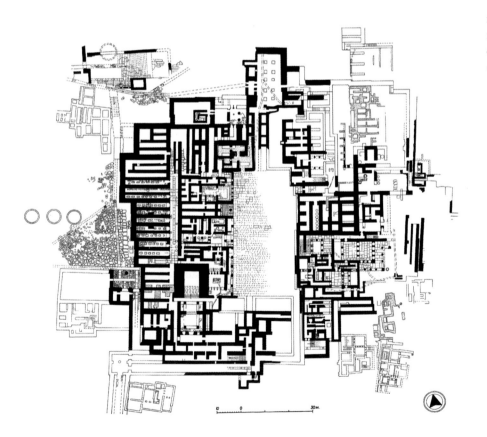

PLAN OF KNOSSOS PALACE: A community center for 100,000 people at its peak

just don't know the answer. Evans thought he had discovered the throne of a king, perhaps the legendary King Minos himself, but Minoan art suggests something else. Women appear as priestesses and goddesses; men worship and serve them. Men have simple clothing; women have elaborately embroidered layered skirts, tight bodices designed to create cleavage, with their breasts lifted—and exposed. Gold earrings and bracelets dangle on the women; rouge and red lipstick adorn their faces. Women seem to be able to go freely outside without protection or supervision of men, picking flowers, carrying fruit baskets, and watching spectacles in crowds that were not segregated by gender.

Each of the palaces, or building complexes, may have sustained as many as 17,000 people or more, who lived inside them as well as in the countryside around them. Knossos was not the only place on Crete with complex monumental architecture, for Phaestus, Malia, and Kato Zakros also have these features, all on the east side of Crete. In addition, a port city has been excavated at Kommos facing south toward Egypt, and there is also evidence of smaller settlements. So there was likely a network of "palaces"—centralized economic redistribution centers—in contact with each other and collaborating when needed. Crete is the largest island in the Aegean, situated south of the Cyclades; it served as a way station between Egypt, the Near East, and mainland Greece and was undoubtedly a busy hub.

As people brought trade goods and produce into palace compounds, the products would be counted or weighed and recorded on clay tablets. Perishable goods were held on-site in vast storage areas, refrigerated by being placed in large ceramic barrels set into the earth. Imagine farmers and craftsmen coming into the palace from their country homes, offering their products to the compound, recording how much they brought and being permitted to take in exchange an assortment of supplies they would need. This place would serve as a meeting ground, a hub, a communications center, and a place to visit with old friends or make new ones.

THE FRESCOES AT KNOSSOS

A S MICHELANGELO USED ON THE Vatican's Sistine Chapel, fresco is a technique of wall painting in which the artist applies mineral-based pigments to wet plaster. Color soaks into the wall itself, rather than being applied to a dry surface. Over time, when these walls break down and fall, the plaster crumbles into pieces that retain the color deep into the surface.

The wall paintings in Minoan palace complexes show details of daily life, as well as the exuberant and imaginative spirit of the people. The life-size humans are shown picking flowers, fishing, dancing, walking in ritual procession, and doing other peaceful things. The men and women are eternally young, men painted with dark skin, women always white. The way they are dressed tells us about their lifestyle, and their level of technology.

Some walls are painted with plants and wildlife, showing the Minoans' love of nature, painted with an almost scientific appreciation and careful observation. Some rooms—such as one in which a blue bird lands momentarily on a rocky outcrop, amid wild roses, irises, and tall grass—give viewers the sensation of standing in an open-air meadow. Another, the room of the blue monkeys, portrays animals not found on the island of Crete, but perhaps seen by travelers to Egypt and Africa. And then there are the fantasy creatures like the griffins and Minotaur, ancient mash-ups between birds and mammals or animals and humans.

Other frescoes produce the illusion of being deep in the ocean, creating a fantasylike experience with dolphins for the people who worked

FRESCO, KNOSSOS: Eight youths in uniform approach a priestess.

or slept in that room. As beautiful as the rooms are, it seems these people treasured being outside in the Mediterranean sun.

Evans insisted on restoring as much as he could of the palace once the excavations were over. For 20 years or so after the rooms were excavated, workmen poured concrete, added wooden beams, and painted walls in bright colors, often using the smallest fragments of plaster as the basis for painting entire walls. Piet de Jong, a Dutch artist, supervised the reconstructions and may be blamed for enhancing, shall we say, the plaster fragments that so tantalized him.

The room of the dolphins, for example, which makes one feel one is in the middle of an aquarium, may be an entirely erroneous reconstruction. Scholars now believe that the painted plaster fragments of the dolphin frescoes originated as the flooring for a room one story above that collapsed and landed there. Most of it represents the work of de Jong.

The fresco called the Prince of the Lilies is also controversial. The image of this noble-looking man is still the symbol of Knossos on the ashtrays, shot glasses, and postcards on sale at the site. In the early publications, and for many years, people thought that this was a young King Minos or Theseus, and that the painting proved that Minoan Crete was a monarchy. New studies have shown that the prince is really a mix of three different painted figures found in different parts of the room. His head is facing a different direction from his body, for example. All that is original of him is a small piece of his headdress and part of his head—but not the face—and a piece of his thigh. These were "restored" liberally in 1905.

It turns out that even the site's distinctive architectural feature of the tapering red columns with their suspiciously Doric capitals (which originated much later) are also largely fictions.

BLUE BIRDS FRESCO: Birds perch in rocky landscape with verdant wildflowers.

Today it is difficult to tell what is original and what is entirely made up; nevertheless, visitors do marvel at the sense of scale they feel in walking through the complex, with some wings five stories tall. Although modern practice would never allow such irreversible restorations based on such little scholarly certainty, there is no place like Knossos to really imagine what life 3,600 years ago might have been like—more or less.

THE MYTH OF THESEUS
AND THE MINOTAUR

THE CLASSICAL GREEKS KNEW King Minos as the man who established the first empire over the seas; he controlled the Aegean Sea. In Greek mythology, Crete and Knossos were his home and the home of the half-man, half-bull creature called the Minotaur, kept in a labyrinth cage.

Minos's wife, Pasiphae, had mated with a bull sent by Zeus. Embarrassed by the behavior of his wife and her monstrous child, he hid the Minotaur deep inside his palace inside a labyrinth to prevent its escape. The Minotaur fed on humans, and when King Minos ran out of enemies to feed it, he sent for Minotaur food from Athens. According to the legend, the people of Athens were obliged to send into the labyrinth seven boys and seven girls for the beast to devour every year. Many heroes tried to find their way through the labyrinth to kill the Minotaur and put a stop to this barbaric practice, but none had succeeded. They all died either from being eaten or by getting so lost in the labyrinth that they starved to death. The Athenian hero Theseus sailed to Crete

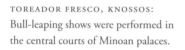

TOREADOR FRESCO, KNOSSOS:
Bull-leaping shows were performed in the central courts of Minoan palaces.

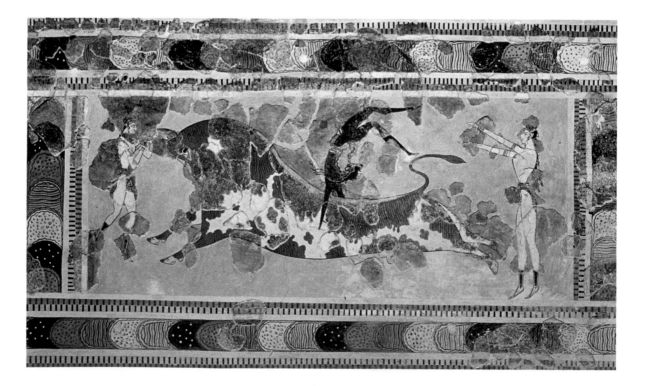

to attempt the task, first seeking local help and intelligence from Minos's lovely daughter, Ariadne. Ariadne gave him a ball of yarn, and held on to one end as Theseus unraveled the other. Winding his way to the center of the labyrinth, he found the beast and killed it. Using the yarn as his guide, he wound up the ball and found his way back to Ariadne's arms.

All of this was thought to be just a myth, until Sir Arthur Evans excavated the site of Knossos, and found bull images everywhere—horns decorating the architecture, paintings showing acrobats leaping over bulls, and stone bull's head drinking vessels with gold-leaf horns. A man could hold the hollow stone bull's head as if to take a drink, and it would look like a mask on him, making him look half man, half bull. But this was no ordinary cup. When filled with red wine, the two drill holes in the nostrils would leak the red liquid to the ground, making the actor look like a dying Minotaur. But the most remarkable correspondence between the myth and the finds is the architecture itself: Knossos had a central court, and a labyrinth of hallways and rooms on all four sides. The plan of the palace looks like a labyrinth.

Another myth related to Theseus and the Minotaur was the story of Theseus's father. King Aegeus was a very early king of Athens, according to legend, and sent his son off to Crete from the promontory south of Athens called Cape Sounion. The ship had two sails, the black one it set off with, and a white one to signal from afar that Theseus was returning successful. King Aegeus waited day after day to see the ship come back. On Theseus's way home from Crete, the ship's crew stopped on the Cycladic island of Naxos to rest and celebrate. Ariadne came along, but got lost on Naxos and Theseus didn't notice that she was gone. Halfway to Athens he discovered that she was missing, and was so upset that he forgot to change the sail from black to white. When King Aegeus saw the sail was black, he feared his son was dead and so threw himself over Sounion's cliff into the sea. From that point on, the Athenians called it the Aegean Sea, named after their beloved king.

There are other versions of the myth, though. In one, Theseus and Ariadne did leave Crete together and spent the night in Naxos, but he departed without her on purpose. In other words, he dumped her. Dionysus finds her on Naxos, grieving, and becomes her rebound; they live happily ever after.

THESEUS SLAYS MINOTAUR: Ariadne and her parents witness the act on a Greek vase, sixth century B.C.

MINOAN GOLD RING, PHOURNI, CRETE: An acrobat does a backflip over a bull.

PALACE AT KNOSSOS

THE DISCOVERY OF Knossos in 1900 was a game changer for classical archaeology. A new field of archaeology of the Aegean Bronze Age was born. Since then, six other sites with Minoan palaces on Crete have been excavated, and we know Knossos was not unique, although likely it was the largest. With 1,400 rooms, the complex is two and a half times larger than others on Crete, occupying 225,000 square feet.

All palaces have paved roads, central courtyards, multistory structures, a throne room, storage rooms, and archives for records. The bull-leaping shows and rituals were performed in the central courtyard. The roofs were decorated with horns of consecration, seen upper left. Inside all Minoan palaces, excavations found vases bearing octopus, nautilus, ivy-leaf, double-axe, and other unmistakably Minoan designs, as well as bronze tools, seal impressions, stone vases, gold jewelry, seal stones, and more.

MINOAN POTTERY

DARING, SKILLFUL, CHARMING—Minoan ceramicists experimented with color, shape, technique, and decorative motifs that continue to delight. On some vases, flowers in full bloom, made of clay, were attached to the sides. On another piece of pottery, a pitcher with painted nautilus designs seems to have grown spines like those of a sea urchin.

In Crete, around 1800 B.C. the potters were making vessels, known today as Kamares ware, with a dark background and sometimes appliqué floral attachments. Later vases were clay colored with brown or black representations of nature painted and glazed on the surfaces.

Sea creatures and plants recur as motifs, with the octopus being the most characteristically Minoan decoration. Dynamic flowing limbs with varying sizes of suckers hug the vessels. Large eyes stare back at the viewer from the center of the vessel's body. Marine life, appropriately, tends to decorate closed-necked and narrow-necked jars, pitchers, ewers, and flasks designed to hold liquids. Lilies and wild grasses often decorate storage jars for dry goods. Talented Minoan artisans painted humans on their walls, but never on their pottery.

THE UNDECIPHERED LINEAR A TABLETS

LINEAR A
TABLET

THE MINOANS DEVELOPED the first writing system in Europe around 1700 B.C. The 3,000 clay tablets found at Knossos fall into two categories: a Minoan script called Linear A, and one used by Mycenaeans, who probably took over the palace in 1450 B.C., called Linear B. Linear A, still undeciphered, has 90 symbols that each stand for a syllable rather than a letter. Additionally, some simple drawings serve as logograms, such as a picture of a cup instead of spelling it out. Linear B has been deciphered—it's an early form of Greek. What makes deciphering Linear A so hard is that scholars don't know what language the script records. The Linear B tablets noted the goods brought to the palace and to whom they were redistributed. The purposes of the Linear A tablets were probably similar. The tablets were inscribed with a stylus, then left to dry. They were temporary records, and could be submerged in water to erase their content. The fire that destroyed Knossos baked them.

PITCHER
Barnacles and sea urchin spines
complement marine life designs.

BEAKED JUG
Older-style Kamares ware has curvilinear
abstract designs on a black background.

CRATER
A large punch bowl on a stem has
appliques of clay flowers in full bloom.

PITCHER
Floral style jug decorated with elegantly
drawn grasses found at Phaestus

FLASK
The octopus wraps around the canteen,
as if protecting the water inside.

THE MOTHER GODDESS, HER PRIESTESSES, AND THE ROLE OF WOMEN IN MINOAN CRETE

LINEAR B TABLET: Economic record from Knossos

FAIENCE FIGURINE "SNAKE GODDESS"

Dᴵᴰ ᴡᴏᴹᴱɴ ʀᴜʟᴱ ᴄʀᴇᴛᴇ? Though some may debate to what extent, there is little doubt that women had primary responsibilities in religious ritual, and possibly in the political realm, too. The imagery of Cretan art shows a female-dominated world, both in daily life and in the religious imagination. Frescoes, figurines, and engravings on gemstones and gold rings show mother-goddesses who have male attendants and worshippers. Females are larger than males, with fancier clothes and a central place in scenes. Females perform sacrifices, lead processions, and enter the sacred temples in these scenes far more often than men. Figurines made of a glass paste called faience depict women with tall hats that may signify prestige, carrying snakes. They are known as the snake-goddesses—although priestess, goddess, or queen? We cannot be sure. In Linear B tablets, a goddess named Potnia is the most frequently mentioned. Her name means "mistress."

As women seem to be worshipped and obeyed, and serve as priestesses in ceremonies, think back to that throne room. At the time when Sir Arthur Evans excavated Knossos, the main Greek myth associated with Crete placed a male on that throne, King Minos, so Evans assumed that the palace had a king. Without that myth, however, there is no other evidence that men were dominant in any way. Recent research reinterprets Minoan palaces as economic redistribution centers, with clans (extended families) sharing space inside and outside the compound as a collective. Making decisions together for mutual benefit, these families organized their economy, shared resources, and celebrated festivals together. The throne room with benches for seating 30 may have had representatives from those families in council, rotating the leadership and the throne. Female heads of clans could have been these representatives as plausibly as men. Studying the ancient Greeks always causes us to reexamine our assumptions about what is "normal" in society, and although there is no consensus, many scholars are now leaning toward matriarchy in the period from 1700 to 1450 B.C. on Crete.

RITUAL SLAUGHTER AND SACRIFICE

OUR BEST EVIDENCE for Cretan religion and also for the idea of matriarchy comes from a brightly painted limestone sarcophagus, discovered near a modern village called Hagia Triada ("Holy Trinity") near the Minoan palace of Phaestus.

The painting shows a ritual in progress. From right to left, we see a man wearing a sheepskin skirt carrying a goat for sacrifice. Next, a robed man plays a seven-stringed lyre. In front of him, two women carry buckets of blood toward the left to pour into a larger bucket placed between two double axes on tall columns. The women wear special headdresses and have wing-shaped ribbons hanging down. Such scenes are colorful and intriguing clues that bring to life the archaeological sites most visited on Crete today.

FRESCO, KNOSSOS: Women under a blue tree in the "Sacred Grove and Dance" fresco

THE BURIED CITY OF AKROTIRI

SAILING INTO PORT AT SANTORINI on a cruise ship is a breathtaking experience. Cliffs with five red and brown ribbons of pumice and ash rise above, with the picturesque, whitewashed towns of Thera and Oia at the crest. A donkey path or funicular are your only options to ascend from the sea. In the Early and Middle Bronze Ages, it was not so. The island was an oval, not the C shape we observe from the satellite images today. Santorini was then (and is still) a live, active volcano. Santorini is the only place on earth where people live right on the caldera, the volcano's crater. The main town is called Thera; Santorini is the Latin crusader name, based on the island's worship of St. Eirene (say it out loud three times fast, to see the connection).

When Santorini's volcano erupted in 1628 B.C., it forever changed the island and the lives of those who inhabited it. Archaeological excavations began on Santorini in 1967, resulting in spectacular finds of a vibrant civilization that resembles life on Minoan Crete, but that disappeared almost overnight. Villages and cultivated fields, springs and grazing grounds in the heart of the island were blown to dust by a catastrophic eruption 40 times greater than that of Mount St. Helens in the United States in 1980. Around the edge of the caldera, preserved because they were well above sea level, are the remarkable remains of an idyllic ancient city now called Akrotiri.

The excavators at Akrotiri faced technical challenges similar to those their Italian counterparts met at Pompeii, another ancient city buried in ash by an erupting volcano. The ash settled in quickly, soft as snow, then solidified as a filling like soft clay, penetrating every crack and crevice, holding together the walls some three stories tall and preserving the

BOXING BOYS, SANTORINI: Two youths, heads shaven except for a few long locks, wear belts and boxing gloves.

fresco surfaces and furnishings inside. Over time, wooden beams and tables or chairs disintegrated, but the solidified ashfall held their places as cavities in those exact same shapes. Using concrete or plaster to fill those cavities, archaeologists recovered the shapes of chairs and tables from these natural molds, before removing the fill and working their way down to the floors.

As at Knossos, most wall surfaces were painted with active scenes—especially lively natural vistas and women in prominent situations. There are antelopes, monkeys, and swallows, along with scenes of boys fishing and boxing, and women picking flowers and papyrus. Thousands of whole jars and pots were found in perfect condition, broken only when earthquakes toppled them from the table to the floor. A few Linear A tablets were recovered along with pottery and artifacts from daily life. Remarkably, no bones or bodies have been found at all, and except for one piece intentionally buried under a floor, no gold. This leads scholars to think that early earthquakes or other signs gave advance warning to the inhabitants and that they were able to escape with their most precious belongings and their lives. Because of the remarkable state of preservation, visitors to Akrotiri can imagine a lively place, where apartment buildings sheltered families and neighbors, and where a triangular open area created space for trade, announcements, decision-making, and entertainment. All of this vanished with the eruption in 1628 B.C.

FISHERMAN, SANTORINI: Nude older youth, locks cut off, returns with successful day's catch.

SPRING FRESCO, SANTORINI: Two swallows are caught in a "kiss," top center, in a wild landscape of rocks and lilies.

WAS SANTORINI ATLANTIS?

IF WE WERE THE villagers who escaped by boat from Santorini in 1628 B.C., and then witnessed the eruption, we would feel intense grief and displacement—then we would begin to tell stories. As time went on, we might embellish, to say that our community had been a model of civic life, resolving conflicts peacefully, with a high quality of life. This story may have been told through the centuries. Plato recounts a trip that Solon the Athenian lawgiver took to Egypt in the early sixth century B.C. An Egyptian priest mocked him, saying "Oh Solon, Solon, you Greeks are like children, you don't even know your own history." Then he told Solon about an ideal prehistoric Greek city that disappeared into the sea—a paradise lost—called Atlantis. Although not all of Plato's details fit perfectly, including the location and the date, it is likely that the eruption of Santorini provided the basis of this tale.

EARTHQUAKES AND VOLCANOES IN THE AEGEAN

THERE HAVE BEEN FOUR MAJOR eruptions of the Santorini volcano, from about 100,000 years ago up to the Minoan-period one in about 1628 B.C. It is still active, with several smaller eruptions in the 20th century. The appearance of the dark little island in the center was so remarkable that it was recorded in 1707, and is now understood to be the post-caldera cone called Nea Kameni. Steam still rises from the surface, and it has a sulfuric smell. Photographs have tracked its growth over the decades.

Geologists explain that Santorini is an island on the midpoint of the Hellenic or South Aegean Volcanic Arc. According to the U.S. Geological Survey, an average of 1,600 earthquakes are recorded for this 310-mile belt annually, some resulting in significant damage. These earthquakes are caused by tectonic plate movement at a rate of up to two inches a year. These deep earth activities produced the obsidian on Melos, which is also volcanic.

When Santorini blew in 1628 B.C., the plume shot up over 22 miles high and dispersed ash and tephra throughout the Eastern Mediterranean. The volcano left deposits of white pumice and ash on Santorini up to 160 feet deep.

At the northeastern tip of Crete is a Minoan site called Palaikastro, about 100 miles from Santorini, where archaeologists found a layer of ash from the eruption, as well as evidence of a tsunami shortly following, before the palace recovered. The impact of the tsunami and climactic damage to Crete, however, was not as extreme as it was once thought to be. In older books the eruption of Santorini is blamed for the decline and fall of the Minoans in 1450 B.C., and even for the fall of the Eastern Mediterranean network of civilizations in the Late Bronze Age, about 1250 to 1177 B.C. The new eruption date of 1628 B.C., based on carbon-14 data, means that these catastrophes must be explained in other ways.

VOLCANIC ERUPTIONS: Oil painting shows exodus across the Aegean Sea as Santorini erupts in 1628 B.C.

The village of Akrotiri was situated on the north coast of the island, and when the crater formed, the village was still on land, buried but intact. Modern farmers had hints that something remained there when their hoes hit the tops of walls and potsherds littered the ground. In 1967 an international team went to Santorini to explore Akrotiri. One member, Emily Vermeule, described the first two days at Akrotiri for *The Atlantic* in December of that year: "The first afternoon we had been confident that nothing would happen for a day or two while the upper layers were thinned. By nine o'clock the next morning a workman was picking white crumbs off a wall. These were the first Thera frescoes . . . A few hours later we could not turn around without hitting plaster—on walls, fallen from the ceiling, coated around mysterious constructions with wooden poles at the corners . . . The richness of the site lent it a certain madhouse quality, and the frescoes were the worst . . . We were afraid to clear the walls to the floor level lest they should fall down. For this year, we thought it best to pretend we had never seen the plaster walls of Akrotiri. We covered the whole trench up for the winter."

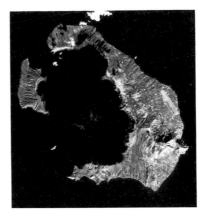

NASA VIEW FROM SPACE: This satellite image shows the volcanic crater and oval shape of Santorini.

VOLCANIC ACTIVITY: An engraving from 1866 shows emergence of Nea Kameni.

THE MYCENAEANS

THE PALACE AND THE CITADEL

THE MYCENAEANS WERE AMBITIOUS and daring, both in their architectural and engineering feats and in their legendary exploits. These were the people that later generations would say lived in the Age of Heroes.

The Minoans had reached their peak between 1750 and 1400 B.C., while at the same time on the Greek mainland, a new power was on the rise: the people now called the Mycenaeans. The rich grave goods discovered at Mycenae prove that by 1650 B.C., they were a wealthy powerhouse. Some two centuries later, these mainlanders took over Crete, using the Minoan palaces to further their own agenda. They kept track of resources by inscribing clay tablets in Linear B, an early form of the Greek language still in use to this day.

The citadel of Mycenae still appears formidable, and inside, a surprise awaits: At first we get a glimpse, and then around the bend, a full

MYCENAE RECONSTRUCTION: The fortified citadel of Mycenae as it may have looked in 1250 B.C.

view of the earliest large-scale sculpture in the Aegean. Three massive stone blocks frame the entrance. The grand doorway is crowned by a triangular limestone plaque on which was carved two lionesses in heraldic pose, flanking a column upheld by an altarlike podium, on which the lions rest their front paws. The heads of the lions, now missing, were fashioned from either a contrasting color of stone or some more precious material. Some scholars have suggested that this may have been the "coat of arms" for the ruling family.

The focal point of all Mycenaean palaces was the "megaron," or throne room. To enter the megaron, visitors had to pass through two vestibules first, where we think sentries and guards protected the king, and where petitioners could nervously wait for their appointments. The throne would be on a side wall, rather than directly in line with the entrance, so no one with a bow and arrow could take an easy shot. Four columns in the center held the corners of a skylight that allowed smoke from the hearth to escape.

Like an early Wizard of Oz, the king enhanced his mystique with theatrical tricks, dazzling and terrifying awestruck visitors. They would first hear the crackle of a roaring fire and smell the burnt wood, perhaps sprinkled with incense. The smoky haze disoriented their

LION GATE, MYCENAE: Heraldic lionesses without heads perch on a podium framing a column.

THE LION GATE

IN 1801, LORD ELGIN dispatched two of his men to explore the Peloponnese, about the same time that his team began their expedition that would result in taking half the sculptures from the Parthenon to London, where they remain on display at the British Museum. One of the two explorers he dispatched, Philip Hunt, wrote this report on the Lion Gate to Lord Elgin: "No description can convey an adequate idea of the massive stones which compose its [Mycenae's] walls. The Ancient Greeks supposed them to have been the work of the Cyclops, as well as two colossal Lions in bas-relief over the Gate Way; and which still remain in this original situation. The block on which they are sculptured is too gigantic and too distant from the sea to give any hopes of being able to obtain so renowned a monument of the Fabulous ages." The lionesses, originally placed there around 1250 B.C., remain on guard to this day.

vision, causing them to wonder if the mythical animals painted on the walls were real, imagined, or something between. Zigzag lines in yellows and reds made the columns appear to tremble. Floors painted in great square panels made the large room seem even larger, and made supplicants feel even smaller. Over time, the Greeks further developed and leveraged this talent for creating spaces that heighten sensory perceptions and elevate the ordinary to the extraordinary.

The wealthiest Mycenaeans were buried in beehive-shaped tombs made of tremendous stones, put together in a style called Cyclopean masonry. The builders laid the trimmed stones in rough courses, with pebbles and rocks filling in the chinks. These stones could weigh a hundred tons, and building crews dragged them over ground, sometimes from faraway quarries. To build a beehive tomb, the masons cut into a natural hill. They excavated the mound, course by course, dropping the stones into place, supported by the earth in the hill. Only the dome needed to be built up above the mound's surface. These were the smallest stones, coiling around until the circle closed. The tomb was then covered over with dirt.

GOLD BODYSUITS, MYCENAE: Sheets of gold covered the bodies of two children buried in the shaft graves.

The largest and most impressive beehive tomb from Mycenae is nicknamed the Treasury of Atreus, after the legendary king who was the father of Agamemnon. The intricately carved green stone half-columns and red stone veneers that framed the majestic doorway were quarried some 60 miles away, a great expense for something that would be buried forever, immediately after it was built.

The buried dome was supposed to remain hidden forever. Unfortunately for the Mycenaeans, later Greeks and then Romans usually figured out what these unnatural mounds really were, and robbed these tombs, taking out a top coil of stone from above the mound, then shimmying down a rope through the hole. When archaeologists excavate them, there are only bones and broken pots, but hardly anything of value, even though Mycenaeans buried nobles with treasure.

The wealth and means to assemble large teams of men to honor the dead is impressive. Considering that such tombs appear near every major Late Bronze Age settlement between 1500 and 1200 B.C., and that archaeologists have discovered 127 of them, we must imagine a common culture, where the elite knew each other, visited each other, and competed with each other even in death.

BEEHIVE TOMB, MYCENAE: *(opposite)* Interior of the so-called Treasury of Atreus with its corbeled vault

SHAFT GRAVES AT MYCENAE

A<small>T MYCENAE, A NEW BUILDING PROJECT</small> around 1250 B.C. strengthened the fortifications, installed the Lion Gate, and extended the city walls so that a venerable cemetery already four centuries old would lie safely inside the walls. This signifies that the people living in Mycenae remembered their ancestors who had died so long ago, and wanted to protect even the dead from potential invaders. But it wasn't just the dead they were protecting; these weren't average citizens buried in these graves, and their burial rituals apparently included interring valuables with the bodies. When the German archaeologist Heinrich Schliemann uncovered the graves in about 1875, he found extraordinary buried treasures—gold death masks, daggers with intricate ornamentation, long bronze swords with golden hilts, stone vessels imported from Egypt, gold disks once sewn to their shrouds, carved gemstones in the Minoan style, and so much more, now on display in the National Archaeological Museum in Athens. Men and women and even children rest in these so-called shaft graves, buried with personal effects that signify great prestige and wealth. The two children wore small gold bodysuits. Several men had those elaborate gold death masks, along with gold beads and buttons. Some wore diadems, crown-like golden headbands. The women wore bronze crowns with gold ornaments, gold bands around their heads, silver earrings, and necklaces with pendants or with beads of silver, gold, amethyst, carnelian, and even amber from the Baltic.

GOLD DIADEM, MYCENAE:
Gold headdress from Grave Circle A

The most famous artifacts found in the shaft graves of what is known as Grave Circle A are the golden death mask Schliemann called "the face of Agamemnon"—wrongly, it turns out—and the solid gold "cup of Nestor"—probably buried centuries before the time of that legendary king. (A second cemetery called Grave Circle B was discovered nearby in 1951.)

Even though the 19 people buried there were not the heroes of Homer's epics, the fantastic finds in the shaft graves provide clues about the values of these people. Wealth represented status and power. For these Mycenaeans, being a warrior was paramount, and to be buried with one's armor and weapons, as well as all that gold, was a great honor for those who had achieved the highest ranks of society.

WHO IS BURIED IN GRAVE CIRCLE A?

WHEN SCHLIEMANN EXCAVATED the Mycenaean shaft graves and found his first golden death mask, he famously wrote, "I have gazed upon the face of Agamemnon." The problem was, King Agamemnon's generation lived four centuries later than these people.

So if that wasn't Agamemnon, then who is buried in grave circle A? How did they become so wealthy? Some scholars hold that they were Indo-Europeans who entered Greece in the Early Bronze Age. Others believe they are indigenous to the region. Either way, one thing appears certain: They became wealthy serving as middlemen in a metals trade that extended from the Near East through Cyprus and Crete to the mainland. From Greece these valuable materials were shipped off to Italy and the Western Mediterranean beyond.

GOLD
DEATH MASK

GRAVE CIRCLE A, MYCENAE: The shaft graves terrace is protected by the curved fortification wall.

THE WARRIOR AND THE MILITARY INDUSTRIAL COMPLEX

THE MYCENAEANS WERE PROUD warriors, and their artwork is infused with images of soldiers. The walls of their palaces were painted with battle scenes, giving them a very different feel from Minoan palaces. For one thing, the paintings show the big business of manufacturing armor and equipment for battle. At Tiryns we see two warriors, marching with two spears each. They wear short tunics with cap sleeves, which is a little unusual, as they don't seem to be wearing their armor. A typical outfit for warriors in Mycenaean times would include bronze chest plates that wrapped around the shoulders to protect the upper arms. The warriors wore heavy tunics with skirts or kilts woven of sheep's wool, so the thick fabric protected them from the waist to the upper thigh. Bronze armor known as greaves protected the front of the legs from the knees to the shin, and leather boots covered their feet. These warriors also carried large round shields, although they also sometimes used figure eight–shaped and large rectangular shields, too. They carried long spears, with swords or daggers hanging from their waists.

Their helmets usually had a crest, and sometimes a horn in front, to make the warrior look even fiercer. Some warriors used helmets made of boars' tusks. Such helmets are painted on walls at Santorini and much later at Pylos. One helmet may have required 40 tusks, and considering how dangerous it was to kill a wild boar, such helmets symbolized great strength as well as conspicuous expense. More than 50 Late Bronze Age graves have at least one boars' tusk plate from such a helmet.

Homer's description in *The Iliad* of a boars' tusk helmet is remarkably accurate: ". . . he too put over his head a helmet fashioned of leather; on the inside the cap was cross-strung firmly with thongs of leather, and on the outer side the white teeth of a tusk-shining boar were close sewn one after another with craftsmanship and skill; and a felt was set in the center." In Homer's day these helmets had been out of use for at least 400 years. No one alive had ever seen one. Detailed stories of the Age of Heroes were passed down orally through the centuries until Homer's version pulled them all together for posterity.

GOLD RING: Two men hunt deer by chariot. Minoan-style ring has a violent Mycenaean theme.

INLAID DAGGER, PYLOS: A Mycenaean blade inlaid with gold and silver, with a Minoan nautical theme. FRESCO, TIRYNS: (*opposite*) Two soldiers on patrol carry short spears.

BRONZE AGE FOOD BANKS

IN EVERY SOCIETY, people pass down traditions through food, and the Mycenaeans were no exception. Their recipes reflect their local environment and tell us a lot about their culture. The Greek diet has had many influences over the centuries, but the core has remained the same since the Bronze Age: the "Mediterranean triad" of olives, grapes, and wheat. Without a good supply of these three essentials to make oil, wine, and bread, the redistribution systems of Minoan and Mycenaean palaces would have collapsed. To sustain populations of 17,000 or more meant they needed substantial storage facilities with good accounting systems and security from thieves, vandals, and varmints.

Mycenaean palaces were political centers, communications centers, and social centers, but also economic redistribution centers. People brought in whatever they grew or made, got receipts for it, and took home what they needed. The Linear B archive records these exchanges, as well as landholdings, work crew assignments, and other administrative information. It was vital that the storage holdings were always kept full in order to satisfy people's requests. The palace economy depended on the cooperation of people to bring in their goods to the center.

This is best seen at Knossos, during the phase when the palace of Minos was under Mycenaean control. These clever people maintained rather ingenious ancient refrigerators, in the form of great storage rooms. These rooms had rows of enormous jars, set deep into the ground, mostly submerged except for the shoulder and neck of the barrel. Grains, nuts, olive oil, wine—almost anything could be stored inside, protected from pests by lids with wax seals. The jars stayed nice and cool inside because they were buried so deeply.

Some of these barrels are plain but others have modest decorations. Molded ribbons were often applied by rolling a coil of clay and attaching these to make ridges on the body of the barrel. The most common decoration is a rope motif. Strap handles or loops were attached at certain key points around the jar as well. Real ropes would slide through those loops so that workers could maneuver them into their positions for

FRESCO, MYCENAE: Discovered in the cult center, this goddess or priestess carries shafts of wheat.

transport or set them into the ground. When full of liquid, these barrels could weigh up to a ton, so maneuvering them was quite difficult. Mostly they stayed in the ground.

Inside Mycenaean palaces people made products out of the raw materials that were brought in from the countryside. We can look at one industry that took off in the Late Bronze Age—perfumes. Scented creams and perfumes were popular on Cyprus and Crete from the Middle Bronze Age, but the mainland remained a stinkier place until about 1450 B.C., when Mycenaeans and Minoans had direct contact with each other on Crete. Only then did tiny juglets of scented oils begin to be buried with the Mycenaeans. Linear B tablets say that Pylos was a major perfume-manufacturing center. By the 14th and 13th centuries B.C., Mycenaean juglets and jars were found in Eastern Mediterranean and Egyptian sites. This means the quality and scale of production in Greece was so high that they could export perfumes, and their distinctive painted jars were recognized as containing the Mycenaean brand.

STORAGE JARS, KNOSSOS: Ropes were once passed through the handles for moving them.

ENGINEERING FEATS

LTHOUGH THE MINOANS WERE skilled engineers, channeling fresh water from the streams to their palaces, evacuating waste water through secondary channels, and mastering the art of building sturdy walls and floors five stories tall, the Mycenaeans went even further. At Mycenae, Argos, Tiryns, and Midea in southern Greece, it's easy to observe the Cyclopean masonry, beehive tombs, and architectural ingenuity of the palaces. One can still cross over streams and gullies using Mycenaean bridges that are 3,300 years old, and hike on paths that once were paved Mycenaean roads. Mycenaean palaces are forts, surrounded by monstrous walls that can be more than 50 feet tall and 47 feet thick in places. The classical Greeks who saw them called it Cyclopean masonry, because only a giant Cyclops could have made them. They have one or two narrow gates that are defensible, with tall towers above from which boiling oil and arrows might be hurled. But once inside, there are features that resemble the Minoan palaces, with a throne room, wall paintings, religious spaces, manufacturing zones, storage space for rows of refrigeration jars, and more. At Tiryns, the storage rooms were made using Cyclopean masonry and corbeled vaults. The stones are laid in courses that gradually lean in, meeting at a peak. These relatively narrow hallways stayed nice and cool.

Water was available from springs, but the Mycenaeans also engineered cisterns or great basins to collect rainwater. At Mycenae they dug a long tunnel into the hillside to reach underground springs from inside the fortification walls, so that if they were attacked, they would never run out of water or have to leave the citadel to fetch it. Visitors at the site today use flashlights (usually on cell phones) to climb down the windy, narrow unlit staircase to see the ancient springs. The corbeled vault is high overhead at first, but as one descends, the ceiling drops. There are no modern handrails, and the steps are uneven, worn with footsteps from

TIRYNS: Vaulted passageways in the palace at Tiryns served as storage chambers.

BATHTUB AT PYLOS

AN ANCIENT POWDER ROOM

KEEPING CLEAN WAS important to the elites of mainland Greece in the Late Bronze Age. Linear B tablets record 66 bath workers at Pylos. One Linear B tablet inventoried bathing items: "three drainable tubs for bathwater, three water jars, three boiling pans, two amphoras, one hydria [water pitcher], seven bronze jugs." One excavated bathroom at Pylos, room 43, still has the built-in ceramic tub intact. Another similar bathtub was excavated at the Mycenaean palace at Thebes; at Knossos, from the Mycenaean phase, the so-called "queen's megaron"—a rectangular hall—had a bath as well. A unique room at the palace of Tiryns has a large, square, highly polished stone floor with holes drilled into it for drainage. This is thought to be what is left of an ancient bathing installation. The room probably had wooden benches all around against the walls, like a sauna. A pedestal held the large jar that provided water for a sponge bath or even a shower. Water would be brought in with ceramic jars, and we imagine bath attendants would scrub down the bathers, as at a Turkish bath today.

3,500 years ago. The staircase is just wide enough for one group to descend as others ascend, single file. The air smells moldy, the humidity rises, but it is also much cooler down there. At the bottom, the reward is a trickle of water on a slimy platform. Still, for those who have time to go to the far side of the site, it is the most memorable part of a visit to Mycenae.

Beehive "tholos" tombs are tremendous burial installations, made of the type of Cyclopean masonry used in fortification walls. The interiors were conical domes, with narrowing circles of stone bricks tapering to a central point. More than a hundred beehive tombs dot the countryside, some quite elaborate, such as the so-called Treasury of Atreus, which had a secondary chamber, too. A long forecourt brought the attendees of the funeral into the chamber, where they left behind the body, the grave goods, and ritual offerings. Afterward, all of it was filled in with soil. Because so much work was involved in constructing these graves, and then they were intentionally buried in earth, they are markers of conspicuous consumption, wealth, and prestige.

BRONZE AGE INTERNATIONAL AFFAIRS

OVER THE THOUSAND-YEAR PERIOD between 2200 and 1200 B.C., the Greeks went from exploring each other's islands in the Cyclades in fishing boats to creating a super network for trade and communications among the islands, Crete, the mainland, and even to Egypt and the Near East. Imagine concentric circles expanding out from the Early Bronze Age Cyclades to the Aegean, then to include Crete, coastal areas of mainland Greece, Cyprus, and beyond. By the third phase of the Late Bronze Age, 1500 to 1177 B.C., the entire Aegean and Eastern Mediterranean were connected in one enormous "world system," with everyone dependent on each other for raw materials and finished products. They went to war and made alliances to keep that connected economy running. By the Late Bronze Age, the mainland Greeks were trading and making regular direct contact with people in what is now Turkey, Egypt, Gaza, Israel, Lebanon, Syria, and Cyprus, as well as trading indirectly with Mesopotamia via Babylon. Their circle had widened.

From the Near Eastern point of view, the Mycenaeans were newcomers on the scene. Egypt was the alpha male of the pack, which included its satellites in Canaan and Syria. The Egyptians had been trading with the Babylonians for quite a while, and with the Hittites, Kassites, and others in Turkey. The Mycenaeans were the last and most geographically distant to join the club that had begun to form back in the 18th century B.C.

The Minoans on Crete were the first Greeks to make it into the international network. The

TOMB OF REKHMIRE: Egyptian tomb painting in Thebes from the 15th century B.C. shows Aegean men bearing gifts including metal vases and an ivory tusk.

Egyptians were eyeing the attractive southern coast of Crete, thinking it would be a great rest stop between Africa and the Mediterranean. And the Syrians probably also wanted a spot beyond Cyprus that would be comfortable, friendly, and whose people would buy the goods they were selling.

In an ancient town named Mari, located on the Euphrates River in modern Syria, palace scribes recorded correspondence for their king. Around 1800 B.C. they specifically praised the quality of Minoan clay vases and leather sandals, as well as the highly prized Minoan bronze weapons, some of which were described as covered with gold and encrusted with lapis lazuli. Apparently Syrians got excited when Minoan ships sailed into port, and ran down to the shore to buy these things. Occasionally, they had buyer's remorse, however. One king dictated to his scribe about his new leather sandals, a product still popular with tourists who visit Greece today: "One pair of leather shoes in the Cretan style, which to the palace of Hammurabi, king of Babylon, Bahdi-Lim [an official] carried, but which were returned." What—the sandals didn't fit? So last millennium?

PROCESSION FRESCO, KNOSSOS: Men display a stone bowl, possibly made in Egypt, and a metal vase.

Evidently, the Minoans really got around. Several of them appear in person, painted on the walls of an Egyptian tomb around 1450 B.C., wearing Cretan clothing and carrying Minoan vessels. One man carries a platter on which rests a bull's head libation bowl, just like the ones at Knossos and in the shaft graves at Mycenae that might have been used for the Minotaur show.

The Mycenaeans got in on the action, too. They had a special relationship with Egyptians, it seems. Egyptian pharaohs sent objects with their own names on them to Mycenae—an honor, considering the Egyptians deemed pharaohs gods. Mycenaeans also traded with the people living in Canaan (modern Israel, Lebanon, and Jordan). Canaanites shipped their transport jars to Greece, and Mycenaean pottery ended up in Canaan. Greece had finally joined the self-organizing trade network of the Near East.

THE ULU BURUN SHIPWRECK

UNDERWATER ARCHAEOLOGY OWES A great debt to sponge divers. For centuries, fathers and sons in Turkey, Greece, and southern Italy have handed down this tradition of holding their breath for extended lengths of time and diving 30, 40, even 50 feet down to collect these useful creatures. Sponge divers are often the first to notice a shipwreck and find ancient statues and trade goods.

In 1982, a young Turkish sponge diver from Bodrum discovered the shipwreck located at Ulu Burun near Kas, on the southwestern coast of Turkey, 140 feet below the surface. Excavations from 1984 to 1994 recovered a 14th-century B.C. cargo ship laden with raw materials and finished products, the oldest known shipwreck, containing goods from seven civilizations in the Aegean and Eastern Mediterranean. It took more than 22,400 dives to excavate the remains of the ship.

Among the most spectacular finds on this one vessel were ten tons of copper and one ton of tin—enough raw material to make bronze armor and weapons for an army of 300 soldiers. The ship that went down at Ulu Burun had 354 complete copper ingots on board. This is how copper is transported as a raw material. Weighing 46 to 63 pounds each, the ingots were stacked on board in a herringbone pattern. Cleaning revealed mysterious markings on 160 of them.

There were also 140 Canaanite jars from Syria, used to transport all sorts of goods, from glass beads to food; 175 blue and purple glass ingots, which are the raw materials for making colored glass objects; and even Egyptian jewelry, including a solid gold scarab inscribed with the name of Queen Nefertiti.

The crew had food on board, either to feed the sailors or to trade, including pomegranates, figs, grapes, almonds, olives, wheat, barley, and some spices identified as black cumin and coriander. The seeds and pits of the fruit were still in the sand at the bottom of the sea after all those centuries. The underwater archaeologists sucked up the sediment with a vacuum, sifted and filtered out these tiny materials, and then analyzed them. Think how small a pomegranate seed is, or the grainy bits inside figs. This archaeological team, led by George Bass and Cemal Pulak, was the most advanced of its time, and did groundbreaking work at Ulu Burun.

Large storage jars like those in the storerooms at Knossos were discovered on board the wreck. The underwater archaeology team was surprised to find that the jars held brand-new stacked cups, bowls, and other vessels from Cyprus and Canaan. Apparently there was a market for the ceramics themselves, not just what they contained. It seems that these large storage jars were the equivalent of the sturdy wooden barrels that have survived many a sea crossing throughout time, these ones bringing fine pottery from the Near East to the Aegean.

The source of the wealth of raw and finished materials on board from Egypt, the Near East, Cyprus, and Greece continues to be a mystery. The question that remains unanswered is whether this ship was sent by one king to another as a gift in exchange for an equally valuable gift in return, or whether this ship belonged to a private merchant and was basically tramping port to port, selling some things and taking on board others, moving in a continuous circle. The enormous value of all the goods becomes all the more impressive when one considers that there might have been hundreds of such ships sailing at the same time. That provides a picture of the robust economy in the Late Bronze Age Mediterranean Sea.

BRONZE AGE SHIPWRECK: Ceramics and a gold chalice cover the seafloor.

GREEK LUXURY ITEMS

TIN AND COPPER, the ingredients for making bronze, were to these economies like the petroleum of the Middle East is to the world today. The tin source was likely in Turkey and Afghanistan, brought to traders in Mesopotamia who moved it to the Mediterranean by ship. The largest copper source was the island of Cyprus, conveniently situated east of Crete and close to the great harbors of Syria, Lebanon, and Israel.

As merchants exchanged basic goods, they also sold more exotic things. Ostrich eggs from Egypt made fine perfume bottles if a craftsman added a neck and mouth. These were so highly prized that they were found buried with the dead at Mycenae. Greeks bought ivory from elephant and hippopotamus tusks from the Egyptians. Mycenaean craftsmen made beautiful figurines with the materials.

The Mycenaeans imported cumin, saffron, and other spices from the Near East, no doubt with marked-up prices. In addition to flavoring food, saffron was used as an aphrodisiac and as a medicinal herb.

More than 30 engraved stones called cylinder seals, made of lapis lazuli, were discovered at the Mycenaean palace at Thebes in Central Greece. The stunning gemstone, which ranges in color from blue to purple, originated in Afghanistan. The seals are about an inch long, and like a cylindrical bead, there is a hole drilled through the center for a leather string or a chain. The engraving is carved into the stone, so that when the cylinder is rolled onto clay, it leaves a raised impression. After careful examination and translation of the texts inscribed upon some of them, it turned out that although they appeared similar, these were variously Kassite, Hittite, Mitanni, and Cypriot, including a seal that bears the name of the Kassite king Burna-Buriash II. In other words, they came from a variety of areas in the Near East. This need not mean that Thebes had direct relations with all of these places, for a single sailor, or one craftsman, might have collected them and brought them to Thebes. At the very least, though, we can say that there was trade and contact between all these people plus with Greece and Egypt.

This is how the Mycenaeans became "rich in gold," the epithet given them by Homer. They became full-fledged members of the super network. By forming alliances within Greece and keeping good relations with the rest of the Mediterranean and beyond, they had many suppliers and a strong customer base to whom they could sell their coveted products.

AMETHYST SEAL STONE
Seal stones were used to stamp clay or wax, but this may be a portrait of a Mycenaean.

OSTRICH EGG BOTTLE
The egg, imported from Egypt, was decorated in Crete or Mycenae using lapis lazuli, faience, and gold.

GOLD CUP
This cup shape, similar to a coffee mug, is found at most Bronze Age sites.

DAGGER
The inlaid daggers were made in Crete and mainland Greece.

GOLD JEWELRY
Beads, pendants, and other ornaments such as these found at Thebes were always in demand.

GOLD BOX
Lions attacking prey decorate this hexagonal gold-leaf box from Mycenae.

THE AGE OF HEROES

THE INDIVIDUAL ACTS OF HEROISM, the expressions of hope and fear, the courage, the light shed on human nature—these are why the long-ago Trojan War is still important, because these struggles are universal.

The Trojan War—when the Greeks attacked the city of Troy in retaliation for kidnapping one of their queens—was their most audacious expedition, remembered to this day. The stories of the daring, clever, and tragic heroes come from a poet named Homer who composed the long poems called *The Iliad* and *The Odyssey*. He lived 450 years after the war between the Greeks and the Trojans supposedly took place. The stories were set in Mycenaean times, based in Mycenaean palaces.

The heroes of the Trojan War each had distinct personality traits, gifts, and vulnerabilities. Ancient and modern readers identify with one or more because we see a resemblance to ourselves and to others we know.

The war started because Menelaus of Sparta left on a business trip, and while he was away, the Trojan prince Paris came to visit. He took Queen Helen back with him to Troy. She is "the face that launched a thousand ships." Menelaus is the type of man who takes his wife for granted while he pursues other goals, losing the woman he realizes he loves only after she leaves him. In *The Odyssey,* set ten years after the Trojan War, we see Menelaus and Helen happily reunited in Sparta. They worked it out.

Agamemnon, king of Mycenae, stood for mission above all. He's the type of man who always thinks he is right, consequences be damned. When the whole army was stranded at Aulis on the way to Troy because there was no wind for their sails, he sacrificed his youngest daughter to appease the gods, and lied to his wife about it. The wind picked up, but Clytemnestra never forgave him. The rest of their story sounds like a soap opera: She took a lover who moved into the palace at Mycenae with their children. On Agamemnon's return from the war, Clytemnes-tra killed her husband inside the palace bathroom; her son and daughter then conspire to kill her; and the son, Orestes, was ultimately tried in court in Athens.

When we first meet Achilles, he seems more like a petulant little boy who just had his toy taken away. As was his right as king, Agamem-non claimed for himself Briseis, a captive princess, but Achilles was already attached to her. Achilles pouts and retreats to his tent. His emotional maturity improves through the epic, and in the end, he dies young in a blaze of glory.

Odysseus, known to the Romans as Ulysses, was the most intelligent and cunning of the Greeks who fought at Troy. He thought up the Trojan horse, from which the saying comes, "Beware of Greeks bearing gifts." He stars in *The Odyssey*, encountering horrifying and magical adversaries as he tries to get home from Troy. He has to rediscover what he really wants in life—to return to his wife, Penelope.

Homer described citadels of Mycenaean kings in Greece, and archaeologists have discovered them right where he said they would be. Did the Trojan War really happen? Probably. If so, the war dates to sometime between 1250 and 1200 B.C.

TROJAN HORSE: The combination of desperation and ingenuity to find a technological solution makes the myth a timeless classic.

EXCAVATIONS AT TROY

Until 1871, when German businessman Heinrich Schliemann began excavating, scholars believed Troy to be a myth, without any basis in fact. What Schliemann found at Hisarlik, a hill at the entrance to the Dardanelles (the strait in northwest Turkey separating Europe from Asia), was a powerful fortress city that matches descriptions in *The Iliad,* with Cyclopean fortification walls, grand gates, and elegant roads. Troy was situated at a strategic crossroads in the northwest corner of the Turkish coastline, at the head of the strait leading from the Aegean into the Sea of Marmara and the Black Sea. It was an ideal spot for cultural interchange with the Eastern Mediterranean network. Excavations over the past 140 years, off and on, have revealed at least nine cities on top of one another, with spectacular small finds and valuable information about the complex relations between the people of Troy with the Hittite world in inland Turkey to their east and the Aegean world to their west. Most recent efforts have focused on the area of the lower town, to uncover what life was like among the common people outside the citadel. The size of this lower town has surpassed all earlier estimates.

Most of what visitors see on the site today is a mixture of the different levels, ranging from the second of Troy's nine cities, which is Early Bronze Age, contemporary with the Cycladic idols culture, to the last of the cities, from the later Hellenistic and Roman times. The theater and Temple of Athena are the most visible buildings, from level nine, dating to the Hellenistic and Roman times.

THE SACK OF TROY: Fear, violence, and turbulence turned their world upside down at the end of the 13th century B.C.

Two of the levels are thought to be the Late Bronze Age city that was sacked by the Mycenaean Greeks when they won the Trojan War. If Homer's epic accurately recalls the destruction of the citadel, the

HEINRICH SCHLIEMANN: FATHER OF MYCENAEAN ARCHAEOLOGY OR GOLD-DIGGING SCOUNDREL?

THE FATHER OF Mycenaean archaeology has a most improbable résumé. Born in 1822, Heinrich Schliemann grew up in poverty in eastern Germany, dreaming of the adventures of Achilles and the Trojan War. How did he raise enough money to fund his digs? He made several fortunes, beginning with his own business selling indigo. In 1850, he learned of his brother's death in California. Dutifully, Schliemann took over his brother's business, which involved buying gold dust and nuggets from miners and selling them in Sacramento to banks, always at a profit. The Crimean War gave him another opportunity to add cash to his coffers by peddling ammunition. In 1858, at age 36, he retired to pursue his passion. In 1871 he began to dig at the site of Hisarlik, which he identified as ancient Troy, and soon thereafter he claimed to have found Priam's Treasure, which is still debated. In 1876 he went on to excavate Mycenae.

Trojan horse may be a metaphor for an earthquake, because Poseidon the Earth-shaker's symbol is a horse. Is it possible that the Greeks couldn't penetrate the walls until an earthquake caused a rupture that allowed them to storm in? Alternatively, the Trojan horse also could symbolize Greek ingenuity. Odysseus proposed the trick as a way around insurmountable odds. We will see the effectiveness of such audacious military proposals in the Persian Wars more than 750 years later on, as well.

In May 1873, Schliemann announced that he had uncovered a remarkable collection of bronze and gold items in the second level of the mound, known as Priam's Treasure. (Priam was the king of Troy in *The Iliad.*) Schliemann whisked most of the artifacts to Athens, where he photographed his wife, Sophia, wearing the jewelry, and then to Berlin, but returned some to the Ottomans in Istanbul in exchange for his excavation permit. The pieces in Germany disappeared in 1945, near the end of World War II, from a bunker near the Berlin Zoo. It was not until September 1993 that the Pushkin Museum in Moscow revealed that Priam's Treasure had been there all along. Does this plunder rightfully belong in Turkey, Greece, Germany, or Russia? This cultural heritage dilemma remains unresolved.

TROY

VISITING TROY IS LIKE traveling
back in time. Five thousand years
of history are visible. People started
living there in the Early Bronze
Age, around 3000 B.C., and built
the first of the nine levels in the
mound. The second level had
Priam's Treasure in it; the sixth
and seventh levels we associate
with the time just before and
during the Trojan War. After
1177 B.C., the palace went into dis-
use. About 500 years later, a new
city was founded on top of that old
palace and the settlers named it
Ilium—Homer's name for Troy.

In 334 B.C. Alexander the
Great and his friends left the
Macedonian army for a long weekend in Ilium, where they took a
grand tour of the places where the
Greek heroes once stood. When
they got to the place where Achilles
and Patroclus were said to have
raced, Alexander and Hephaestion
stripped on the spot, and ran a race
stark naked, much to the surprise
of the local tour guides.

LINEAR B AND THE QUEST TO CRACK THE ANCIENT CODE

A CATASTROPHIC FIRE CONSUMED the Mycenaean palace of Nestor around 1200 B.C., ravaging it so completely that the people of Pylos abandoned the place and never came back. One positive result was that their archive room burned at a very high temperature for so long that it acted as a kiln. Thus, the sunbaked clay tablets stored there, which normally would have been erased and reused the following year, were accidentally preserved as a permanent record of the last days of Pylos.

Hundreds of Linear B texts have been recovered. The bureaucrats were really into everyone's business, tracking accounts, taxes, deployments, work assignments, acquisitions, distributions, and more. They stored personal data, too, giving us details such as the names of individuals and the titles of government roles: lawagetas (people leader), basileus (chief), and wanax (king).

For more than ten years, from 1939 when Carl Blegen, a professor at the University of Cincinnati, discovered the Linear B tablets, the neat rows of symbols inscribed on the tablets were studied but could not be read. World War II brought cryptography to the fore, and many American and English academics served in the war to crack German and Japanese codes. After the war, using these skills, John Chadwick and Michael Ventris attacked the clay tablets with the same enthusiasm they used to fight the Nazis in England's Bletchley Park, with assistance from Emmett Bennett, a professor at the University of Wisconsin, who had also been a code breaker. Their story has been much celebrated.

Also working on the problem, but in quiet obscurity, was Alice Kober, a classics professor at Brooklyn College. While Ventris received

CLAY TABLET, IKLAINA: The three Linear B syllables scratched on the clay tablet from Iklaina form a verb that relates to manufacturing.

the credit for cracking Linear B in 1952, it turns out that he couldn't have done it without Kober's work. From 1940 until her death in 1950, she devoted all her spare time to understanding the ancient script. Using a card system, the professor methodically wrote down each pictogram and character that she saw, with the adjacent symbols for context and the inventory number of the tablet. With 89 different characters, there was a lot to track. She kept this vast collection of slips of paper—more than 180,000 of them—in empty cigarette cartons. When paper was hard to come by during the war, she "borrowed" slips from libraries and church pews, cut up birthday cards, and reused food wrappers. From this work, she discerned patterns in the symbols.

An article on the front page of the *New York Times* on April 9, 1954, announced that Linear B had been deciphered. The ancient script "that for the last half century and longer has baffled archaeologists and linguists has been decoded finally—by an amateur," it said. Ventris was described as an architect and "leisure-time scholar of pre-classic scripts."

Kober died two years before Ventris's breakthrough was announced. Shortly afterward, he died, too, leaving unanswerable the question of how much influence Kober's work had on him. However, her place in the quest to crack Linear B has been restored to memory by several recent books that have assured that Kober's ten years of painstaking work did not die with her.

ALICE KOBER

MICHAEL VENTRIS

IKLAINA: SITE OF THE EARLIEST WRITING EVER FOUND IN EUROPE

TODAY CRUISE SHIPS dock at the western Peloponnesian town of Katakolo for the easy bus ride to Olympia. Two hours' drive south along the coastal road is Pylos, and the village of Iklaina is nearby.

Iklaina was a secondary administration center under control of Pylos. Excavations at Iklaina have uncovered Cyclopean masonry, painted walls, and small finds from the Middle and Late Mycenaean periods. A find in 2010 caught everyone by surprise: a Linear B tablet dating to between 1450 and 1350 B.C. The small tablet—only two inches square—had been accidentally preserved because it was in a heap of garbage that the inhabitants burned, as was their practice. Reportedly, the tablet lists some men's names along with numbers on one side, and a verb that relates to manufacturing on the other. More than that, we cannot yet say.

THE MYCENAEAN PALACE AT PYLOS

THE PALACE OF NESTOR AT PYLOS, a port on the western coast of the Peloponnese in southern Greece, has features similar to those at Mycenae and Tiryns. The king sat in a luxurious throne room at the heart of the complex; storerooms and industrial chambers were arrayed all around. Bright paint covered the floors and walls, and the throne room featured an enormous hearth. The court must have held large banquets, probably with a lot of wine, because in one side room they stored hundreds of goblets of the same size and shape, perfect for throwing a large party. No excavation in mainland Greece has produced as many Linear B tablets as were found at Pylos in 1939, including on the very first day of excavation—an unheard-of occurrence!

Linear B tablets have been found at Tiryns, Thebes, Mycenae, Chania, Knossos, and now Iklaina as well as at Pylos, but only at Knossos and Pylos can we reconstruct the archiving system, because of the sheer quantities preserved. Excavations have produced 3,360 tablets written by at least 100 different scribes at Knossos. At Pylos, we have 1,107 tablets by 32 different scribes. These scribes were specialists, using a stylus to scratch pictograms and symbols in neat rows on the soft clay. They organized the records by placing the tablets in baskets on shelves. In the fire at Pylos that baked those records for posterity, the shelves fell, the baskets burned, and the tablets piled on the floor. When excavated, each tablet's location was recorded, and more than ten years later, when they could finally be read, it became clear that the piles were like filing cabinet drawers, each relating to a different topic.

These short texts individually are rather dull, mostly dealing with accounting and inventories. Villagers from the districts around Pylos used the palace as a warehouse for their agricultural and manufactured products, and it was a marketplace of sorts, too.

Much administrative work was devoted to sorting out land ownership and allotment. Slaves or serfs, assigned to manual labor throughout the districts, are mentioned in the tablets, too. The place was crawling with priests and priestesses, who supervised the religious festivals and managed the religious centers. A warrior class received their armor at the palace and was deployed to posts by the central palace staff. One Linear B tablet recorded that the palace ordered hundreds of men to form a coast guard to protect Pylos in its last days.

PALACE AT PYLOS: *(opposite)* Reconstruction of the throne room. All frescoes here are based on archaeological evidence.

GODS AND GODDESSES OF THE LINEAR B TABLETS

THE GREEKS IN CLASSICAL TIMES believed in many gods and goddesses, which means they practiced what is called polytheism. Many of the classical Greek gods and goddesses, such as Artemis, Hera, Zeus, Poseidon, Hermes, Hephaestus, and Dionysus, are mentioned in the Linear B tablets. They already seem to have the attributes, personalities, and strengths that a fifth-century B.C. Greek would recognize. Demeter is a goddess who represents fertility and crops. By classical times, a fully developed myth features Demeter and her daughter Persephone, who is taken from a meadow by the king of the underworld. Demeter grieves until a deal is struck that her daughter can split her time above and below the earth, an obvious allegory for the cycle of plants in winter. In Linear B tablets, priestesses already regulate Demeter's cult through offerings of grain.

But there is one goddess who is most prevalent in the Bronze Age texts and invisible in the classical ones—a goddess named Potnia, which means something like Our Lady or Mistress. This female power takes her name from the places where she is worshipped, or from what she protects. They called her Mistress of Pylos, Thebes, Athens, and the Labyrinth. They called her Our Lady of the Grain, of Horses, and the Mistress of Animals. Could she be the one represented in Minoan rings and paintings, worshipped and adored on mountain peaks? Did Mycenaeans then continue to worship her, but add in the male sky god Zeus, sea-based Poseidon, and earthbound Apollo to counterbalance the feminine mystique?

One center of Potnia's cult was discovered at Mycenae in a tiny room six feet square, where excavators found at least 16 clay figures ranging from one to three feet tall. The Mycenaeans who worshipped

GOLD PENDANT, AEGINA: Minoan style. A male holds two geese by the neck, straddling three lotuses.

together there created these as focal points for their prayers. The ceramic bodies were made on a potter's wheel like the neck of a vase, but their torsos were modeled by hand to show breasts. They have clownlike faces with dark eyebrows and a prominent pinched nose. Worshippers left doll-like clay figurines as gifts to their divinities. Some women hold their arms up, while others have round torsos from their folded arms. Hundreds of these have been found at all Mycenaean sites. Archaeologists call these Psi and Phi figurines for the shapes of the clay bodies.

CLAY FIGURINES, THEBES: The special hats and upraised arms identify these striped, doll-like idols as priestesses or goddesses.

Offerings left by worshippers were physical signs of their hopes and fears. At the cult center of Mycenae, the archaeologists found three small offering tables and an assortment of small but precious dedications: a scarab with the name of a pharaoh's wife, Queen Tiye; beads made of semiprecious stones like lapis, carnelian, and amber; a small ivory comb; and more.

Religious rituals tend to be passed down through the generations without much change. Yet it is still surprising to see how similar classical Greek religion is to the way these Mycenaeans worshipped some 700 years earlier. Both Mycenaeans and the classical Greeks prayed to many gods, left valuable gifts on altars, and built sacred precincts called sanctuaries.

Sacrificial rituals leave traces as pits and mounds of ash and animal bones. The Bronze Age Greeks sacrificed animals, just as the classical Greeks did, at funerals, festivals, and before going off to war. The Hagia Triada sarcophagus on Crete gave us an idea of the rituals involved in animal sacrifices, with a lyre player performing while buckets of blood were ceremonially poured on an altar. The custom of burning the fat while sharing the meat in communal feasting is reflected in Homer's epics, too. The idea behind the burning fat is that it creates a very dark plume of smoke that would signal the gods above to invite them to watch the ceremonies in their honor.

CLAY BULL: Ceramic figurines of cattle are found all over Bronze Age Greece.

Besides eating animals, the priests examined the animals' liver or entrails to learn what the gods had in store before embarking on military campaigns. Although it seems superstitious to us, these rites provided people with confidence going into a dangerous situation, to know that the gods approved. If what the priest saw in the entrails was inauspicious, the event was delayed or canceled.

KALAPODI AND RELIGIOUS CONTINUITY

Aт THE END OF THE BRONZE AGE, early in the 12th century B.C., all over Greece and Crete the last Mycenaeans exited through the Cyclopean gateways, their oxcarts fully loaded with the family's possessions. After that moment, the palaces were abandoned for at least two centuries, gradually covered over with dirt until they were overgrown and hidden from view. Centuries passed, and then people came back and built a town or sanctuary right on top, oblivious that anything significant was beneath their feet. It is almost as if the later builders at these sites sensed there was something significant about the place where they chose to put their altar or temple, but they couldn't quite remember what it was. They might have seen some Cyclopean masonry there and identified that with the Age of Heroes. It might simply be that the Mycenaeans had situated their buildings on the best part of the site, and the later Greeks looked at the landscape and decided that spot was perfect.

KALAPODI: New excavations show a sequence of continuous worship on the spot from the Bronze Age through the Roman era.

Classical temples that sit directly on top of Mycenaean places include Olympia and the Acropolis at Athens, and the Temple of Poseidon at Cape Sounion at the tip of the Attica peninsula. Even at the oracle of Apollo at Delphi, Mycenaean idols were found directly underneath the Archaic temple, but nothing suggests that people continuously prayed there between the 14th and the 8th centuries B.C.

In all of Greece, only one spot is the exception that proves the rule: Kalapodi.

Located one hour by car northeast of Delphi, Kalapodi was continuously inhabited from the 14th century B.C. to the 2nd century A.D. It was not a city, but rather a sacred place, a shrine. At the end of the Bronze Age, people first gathered around an altar together to worship the gods at Kalapodi, and didn't stop for 1,300 years.

People continuously made animal sacrifices and deposited gifts to the gods there, meaning that local people passed down cultural traditions from the Bronze Age through the Iron Age to the beginning of the Archaic period, when they finally built a temple. When we wonder how Homer, living around 750 B.C., could remember so accurately places and traditions from the Bronze Age, we look to a place like this, where social traditions were so important to people that they passed them on to their children, and those children then taught their own children by bringing them back to this place for the ceremonies that took place several times a year. The people at Kalapodi thought this temple was so significant that they rebuilt it 11 times over the centuries.

Later worshippers named the goddess who protected this place Artemis Elaphebolos, "Artemis the Deer-Shooter." Artemis dwelled in forests and tamed all the animals. The Bronze Age goddess, Potnia, was called Mistress of the Animals. The religious practice of worshipping Potnia in the Mycenaean period might have continued as praying to Artemis here. The excavators believe that Kalapodi was also the classical site of an oracle of Apollo, Artemis's twin brother.

Revering the past and keeping traditions going is a consistent cultural trait of the ancient Greeks. That never stopped them from looking toward the future, though.

SOUNION: Human activities at Cape Sounion begin in the Early Bronze Age lasting through Roman times, but not quite continuously.

THE DECLINE AND FALL OF THE BRONZE AGE CIVILIZATIONS

STORAGE ROOMS, KNOSSOS: Drought in the late 12th century B.C. may have emptied palace warehouses throughout the Aegean, causing a run on the food bank.

For more than 100 years, archaeologists working at ancient sites in Turkey, Syria, Lebanon, Israel, Iraq, Egypt, and Greece found evidence of destruction in the period from 1250 to 1150 B.C. Almost all of the major cities of this era, and a lot of the minor ones too, were burnt down, damaged, or otherwise destroyed, except in Egypt—which was weakened but did not collapse. Some places show earthquake damage that preceded or caused the destruction. In other places, surviving texts mention drought, which would bring famine and disease. And in still others, there is evidence of war, as if the palace or citadel was under siege. In some, there are no bodies or weapons at all, and no precious items either, which suggests that the ancient people simply abandoned the place. Two written works also talk about famine, disease, warfare, and migration around 1200 B.C.—the story of Moses in the Bible, and the Trojan War in Homer's epic tales.

On top of all these terrible problems, there were invaders. The Sea Peoples, as they are called, were a coalition of pirates who came into the Aegean and Eastern Mediterranean between 1250 and 1177 B.C. We know precisely the date when the Egyptians defeated them because the ancient Egyptians covered temple and tomb walls with hieroglyphics. When the Sea Peoples got to Egypt, the pharaoh had already heard about them, and had laid a trap. Writing on the walls at Medinet Habu,

Pharaoh Ramses III (1184–1153 B.C.) declared that he had defeated a coalition of foreigners who had invaded Egypt.

He was especially proud to announce how he, of all the civilizations around him, was the only one to soundly defeat the attackers. On the walls Ramses III writes about the enemy, and then what he did to them: "These lands were united, and they laid their hands upon the land as far as the Circle of the Earth. Their hearts were confident, full of plans. Now it happened through this god, the lord of gods Amun, that I was prepared and armed to trap them like wild fowl . . . I, King Ramses III, was made a far-striding hero, conscious of his might, valiant to lead his army in the day of battle. Those who reached my border, their seed is not; their heart and their soul are finished forever and ever." The year was 1177 B.C. By then, most Mycenaean palaces, plus those on Crete and Cyprus, as well as cities on the coast of Syria and Israel, had already been destroyed.

MEDINET HABU TEMPLE OF RAMSES III: Egyptians fight and defeat the Sea Peoples in 1177 B.C.

This was no war between neighbors. It took the form of shadowy guerrilla-style raids. Who were these invaders? Ramses III explained how his neighbors fell like dominoes, and even names the people behind this disruption: "Lands were disturbed and taken away in the fray at one time. Not one stood before their hands, from the Hittites, Cilicia, Carchemish, Arzawa [southwest Turkey], Cyprus, they were wasted." The pharaoh then names the components of the Sea Peoples, calling them the "Peleset, Tjekker, Shekelesh, Denyen, and Weshesh."

Historians, not the Egyptians, call these pirates the Sea Peoples. The Peleset were probably Philistines from Israel and Lebanon; the Shekelesh might be early Sicilians; the Denyen might be Homeric Danaans from mainland Greece, or even the biblical tribe of Dan. These strange bedfellows might have gotten together originally as a band of pirates who kept building strength as they moved around the Mediterranean. But because women and children were traveling with them, perhaps we ought to think of this as a migration, and the Sea Peoples as looking for land to make a new life for themselves.

Why did the migration start? For one, hunger. A drought from 1250 to 1100 B.C. in Israel, coastal Syria, Cyprus, and even Greece forced people to leave their homelands in search of food.

LESBOS: Drought conditions caused cracked mud and salt pans, as seen along a river channel on the island of Lesbos.

Another contributing factor may have been climate change, possibly a little ice age, which probably caused the drought. The climate change was perhaps exacerbated in some areas by man-made soil degradation and deforestation.

A hungry people suffering from uncooperative weather can become a desperate people fairly quickly, and the result was instability, destruction of cities, and disruption of trade routes. Copper and tin became difficult, if not impossible, to obtain. It would be like North Americans suddenly not having access to gas and oil.

Then, on top of that, the region experienced an "earthquake storm," which was a series of temblors and aftershocks unzipping the South Aegean Volcanic Arc, and possibly the North Anatolian fault line and the Rift Valley fault line as well. Archaeologists point to crooked walls and broken staircases in Bronze Age palaces, from Greece across Turkey and into modern-day Syria and Israel. The Trojan horse may be a poetic metaphor for an earthquake that toppled the walls of Troy.

Given what we know about Mycenaean palaces as economic redistribution centers, it is possible to imagine that internal rebellions brought down the palaces as well. Consider a scenario in which you were a shepherd and customarily brought your wool to the palace to trade for groceries. Because of the drought, the farmers had very little fruit or wheat to bring in. You offer your wool, but there is no food for you to take home. You decide to take your wool back home and barter with neighbors or trade on a black market. If everyone started to bypass the palace in this way, the palatial storage rooms would become quite empty. People would become hungry and angry. An internal rebellion could cause a riot with looting and arson. In fact, such a looting of a palace is perhaps reflected in Homer's *Odyssey,* where Penelope's suitors take advantage of Odysseus's absence to eat and drink him out of house and home.

The Egyptians had trade relations with Crete from 1800 B.C., and called that island "Keftiu." The Aegean islands, from the Egyptian vantage point, were romantically known as "the Isles in the Midst of the Great Green." Around 1600 B.C., the Mycenaeans on the Greek mainland were invited to join the vibrant, dynamic Egyptian-led international trade network spanning the Aegean and Eastern Mediterranean regions, reaching inland as far as Mesopotamia.

The Bronze Age international trade network had been resilient and responsive for centuries, but not necessarily threatened by outsiders. It seems luck ran out at this critical point in the early 12th century B.C. Too many hits came at once, and too many external forces disrupted too many essential elements. The result was catastrophic system failure that brought about the downfall of the Bronze Age in the Eastern Mediterranean.

Life changed dramatically in Greece at the end of the Bronze Age, around 1177 B.C. Nine out of ten Mycenaean sites were utterly abandoned. There was no need for writing because the economy simplified. The age of well-built complexes with 1,000 rooms was over. Survivors fled to the mountains, built small shacks and huts with their clans, and hid from the rest of the world. They remained cut off for about 400 years. We call this catastrophic system failure the beginning of the Iron Age. Later Greeks will look back on the Mycenaeans, and call it the Age of Heroes. ❖

LINEAR B TABLET

RIPPED FROM THE HEADLINES: THE LAST WORDS FROM PYLOS

PYLOS EVENTUALLY WENT up in flames. The fire baked the clay tablets in the archive room. One tablet records military activity of the last week before the catastrophe. A military guard on watch looks to the ocean, under two named commanders with 50 and 80 men, respectively. It's likely the coast guard awaited the dangerous Sea Peoples.

And some anonymous scribe captured the final days of his city: "Thus the watchers are guarding the coast. Command of Maleus at O-wi-to-no: Ampelitawon, Orestas, Etewas, Kokkion Fifty su-we-rowi-jo men of O-wi-to-no at Oikhalia. Command of Nedwatas: Edhemedes, Amphi-e-ta the mara- te-u, Ta-ni-ko. Twenty Kuparissian ke-ki-de men at A-ru-wo-te, ten Kuparissian ke-ki-de men at Aithalewes (and with them the Follower Kerkios). Aeriquhoitas, Elaphos, Ri-me-ne. Thirty men from Oikhalia to O-wi-to-no, and twenty ke-ki-de men from A-pu-ka (and with them the Follower Ai-ko-ta)."

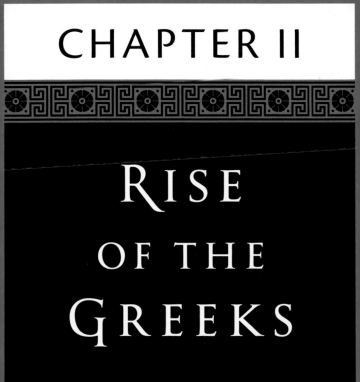

CHAPTER II

RISE OF THE GREEKS

1177 B.C.

Post-Mycenaean migrations,
displacement, poverty

1100 B.C.

Dark Age/Iron Age begins

900 B.C.

Villages become early
city-states

776 B.C.

Olympic Games begin

750 B.C.

Archaic period begins;
Greek Renaissance,
city-states colonize the
Mediterranean; Homer

700 B.C.

Poetry and philosophy
develop; hoplite warfare
standardized

650 B.C.

Coins start to be used;
oracle at Delphi flourishing

600 B.C.

First stone temples, statues;
Solon establishes
Athenian constitution

532 B.C.

Thespis invents
Greek tragedy

508 B.C.

Beginning of democracy
in Athens

STRIVING FOR PERFECTION
1177–508 B.C.

T HE SYSTEM FAILURE THAT DESTROYED THE BRONZE AGE civilizations brought on a dark age that lasted 400 years. From 1200 to about 800 B.C., known as the Iron Age, life was simple, and very hard. People farmed, raised sheep and cattle, and lived with their extended families in small villages. They called the land Hellas and referred to themselves as Hellenes, named for a mythical male ancestor, Hellen. They did not think of themselves as part of a single nation, but as independent regions sharing a common language and culture. This chapter presents the characteristics of Greek culture as it developed from the Iron Age into the Archaic period.

The Iron Age way of life changed around 750 B.C. Homer composed *The Iliad* and *The Odyssey* then; writing began, allowing a flowering of poetry, history, drama, and philosophy. The uniquely Greek styles of painting, sculpture, and architecture emerged, too. The Hellenes formed large cities and experimented with new political systems. Through colonization, Greek culture spread throughout the Mediterranean. City-states developed the Greek style of hoplite warfare. With wealth from conquests, travel, and trade, society became more stratified economically. Political accommodations led to the development of the world's first democracies. This vibrant era from 750 to 508 B.C., called the Archaic period, set the stage for the classical period to come.

DELOS: *(opposite)* Row of marble lionesses protect Apollo's sacred island in the Cyclades. STATUE BASE: *(right)* Athletes play ball on a marble grave marker from Athens.

LIFE IN THE IRON AGE

A FTER THE BRONZE AGE destructions emptied the citadels and palaces, communities turned in on themselves. The Iron Age people of Greece lived in tiny villages for 400 years after the fall of the Mycenaeans in 1177 B.C. Populations were smaller and poorer, and the ruling class seems to have been cut off or cut down. Never again would Greece see cultures based on the hierarchical palace organizations. Now society seemed flat—and that hints at egalitarianism, with at least most men being equal.

From a few families, then extended families, with children and grandchildren, these communities slowly grew. The people farmed, hunted, raised sheep and cattle, and made what they needed to live. Most never left their villages, except for a few traders who went in search of essentials such as metals and tools that couldn't be made at home. Some people obtained gold or silver, but there was no use for it as money, and it ended up buried with them in their graves. The economy was based on barter, where wool could be traded for food, or favors for other favors. The children might fetch firewood, leave it at the neighbor's home, and the neighbor would bring over some vegetables in exchange for their labor. The hierarchy wasn't stratified. It was a relatively even playing field, with most people on the same level—dirt poor.

Because of such poverty, very little architecture or funerary goods have been found from excavation sites of the 12th through 9th centuries B.C. Based on the lack of archaeological remains from the period, historians call this the Greek Dark Ages. Historians also use the term "Iron Age" interchangeably.

FRANÇOIS VASE, DETAIL: Theseus and his excited crew disembark in Attica after slaying the Minotaur.

Throughout Europe at this time there is a transition in weaponry from bronze to iron. In the 12th and 11th century B.C. Iron Age graves in Greece, bronze is still found three times as often as iron, but the use of iron rises greatly in the 10th century and after. The independence and toughness of these people also inspired some to see the strength of iron in them. Writing about 700 B.C., the Greek poet Hesiod says, "For now truly is a race of iron, and men never rest from labor and sorrow by day, and from perishing at night; and the gods shall lay sore trouble upon them. But, notwithstanding, even these shall have some good mingled with their evils."

Hesiod, who was a shepherd and farmer in Boeotia, near Thebes, as well as a poet, helps us to understand better how this society worked. He wrote a magnificent poem called "Works and Days" around 700 B.C., full of (probably

AGRARIAN LIFESTYLE: Most ancient Greeks made their living off animal husbandry or agriculture.

OEDIPUS WRECKS? ROAD RAGE WITH TRAGIC RESULTS

IN THE IRON AGE, travel was dangerous. Stories set in the Bronze Age actually were composed during this period, and reflected that danger. For instance, one evening on a narrow road between Thebes and Delphi, Oedipus saw a four-horse chariot coming toward him, with guards protecting the occupant, who yelled at Oedipus to make way. Oedipus defiantly refused. In what may be the first documented case of road rage, the old man stepped down and they fought. Oedipus killed him, then kept going to Delphi. A few days later he arrived at Thebes and was allowed in, because he was able to answer the riddle of the Sphinx correctly.

The town was in mourning because their king had passed away. Curiously, Oedipus never asked how he died. Jocasta, the queen, fell in love with the young man; they married and had children. The town, though, kept suffering from bad luck. Oedipus returned to Delphi, where the oracle told him he must find the murderer of old King Laius so the curse on the town would lift. Of course, it was eventually revealed that Oedipus himself was the killer, Laius was his father, and he was married now to his own mother. The myth reflects a saying carved on the walls at Delphi: Know thyself.

FOUR-HORSE CHARIOT

GRAVE MARKER: The Dipylon Amphora from Athens is the finest example of Late Geometric pottery of the later eighth century B.C.

unasked-for) advice and harsh criticisms of his brother Perseus, who he saw as a slacker, too proud to do farmwork. From Hesiod we learn about everyday Greek rural life and values at this time, just as Greece was emerging out of its Dark Age. He emphasizes the idea that only hard work helps people achieve the good life, for "between us and excellence [arête] the immortals have put the sweat of our brow." He advises his brother to work hard so that the goddess Demeter will fill his barn, for "working, you will be much better loved both by gods and men; for they greatly dislike the idle . . . if your heart within you desires wealth, do these things and work with work upon work." The poet also warns Perseus not to violate the rules of hospitality, and tells him that Zeus gets angry with a man who "goes up to his brother's bed and commits unnatural sin in lying with his wife . . . or who abuses his old father at the cheerless threshold of old age and attacks him with harsh words." His advice contains all the values of the future Greeks. This includes misogyny, or the general disrespect and oppression of women in Greek society. Hesiod warns, "Do not let a flaunting woman coax and cozen and deceive you: She is after your barn. The man who trusts womankind, trusts deceivers."

The ceremonies for ancient Greek weddings became established at this time, and were simple transactions between the groom and the father of the bride, not love matches. At the wedding, the bride with all her possessions would be brought to the groom's house. The community would follow, and there would be a feast afterward. Ancient Athenian vases from the eighth century B.C. depict a procession of people following the bride in a cart. Fancy weddings involved a long morning getting the bride bathed and perfumed, fixing the bride's hair, and so on, but the ceremony was short and to the point. The groom and the father shook hands, and the deed was done. Then the bride became the mother-in-law's attendant and maid.

There were economic incentives for a man to take a bride. Dowries were involved, and young men were basically bribed to take the girls, who could be 13 to 18 years old. Only Sparta traditionally had girls marry on the older side, but still before the age of 20. The men were about 30 years old when they wed these girls half their age. Naturally, heart-to-heart conversations were tough between couples with such an age and experience gap. This difference may help explain why Greek men preferred to spend time in the company of other men.

Big life events such as weddings and funerals were social and religious rituals. In the Iron Age, Greeks everywhere developed religious practices of prayer, sacrifices, and gift giving to the gods. They set aside land as sacred space. Communities gathered to honor the many divinities of the Greek pantheon, each of which had his or her cult. When we refer to Greek "cults," the meaning differs from modern usage. A Greek religious cult was simply a group of people who worshipped the same divinity. Every city had a main god or goddess, like Corinth had Apollo, or Athens had Athena. There would be numerous other cults as well, and people were free to join whichever they wanted and as many as they wanted. Not all cults had grand temples, but all would have an altar or shrine and a precinct around it marked by a perimeter wall. Everything inside the wall was sacred ground, known as a sanctuary. Religious ceremonies and festivals brought the entire community together to take part in customs and traditions that promoted a common sense of Greek identity.

THE GREEKS LEARN TO WRITE

SEATED SCRIBE

THE GREEKS ADAPTED the Phoenician alphabet in the eighth century B.C. by changing some letterforms to suit their language. Unlike Linear B, they used this alphabet to declare who made or owned precious objects, to accompany dedications in sanctuaries, and to provide information on funeral monuments. They wrote in verse, possibly to make the words easier to remember for passersby. Many dedications were for athletes who won, and the victors would want people to remember the poem and share it back home. The very earliest inscription we have comes from a jug dated to 740 B.C. Right where the neck of the jug meets the shoulders, somebody scratched into the black glaze a phrase in poetic meter that says the jug is a prize "to him who of all those here now dances most exquisitely and best." Even this early, dancing was at the heart of what it means to be Greek—the winner could have been Zorba the Greek's ancestor. Near Naples, at a Greek colony called Pithecoussae, a broken wine cup carried the words, "Nestor's cup am I, good to drink from. Whoever drinks from this cup, him straightaway the desire of beautiful-crowned Aphrodite will seize." The reference to Nestor is a nod to Homer, who described in *The Odyssey* a gold cup once owned by Nestor, king of Pylos. The inscription might also be a magic spell, to "curse" the drinker with physical desire.

RISE OF THE POLIS

AT THE END OF THE IRON AGE, people who lived in small communities near each other began getting together at sanctuaries and working together politically, motivated by a need to defend themselves and their territory by forming armies together. Between 850 and 700 B.C., populations all over Greece grew. Some people who still lived in scattered small hamlets and villages began to move to denser urban centers, the big city. Urban dwellers still needed to eat, so the farms needed to be maintained in the countryside. Markets developed in the centers, where the farmers could trade their products with city folk. The people who continued to live in the villages began to regard the city as their capital. This is how the city-states got their start: The large urban centers plus the neighboring country villages and farmland formed one political unit. This was called a polis, which is defined as the urban center plus the land that supported it, allowing each city-state to be relatively self-sufficient. Thus, the residents of Marathon, living 26 miles from the urban center of Athens, were still

THE ATHENIAN AGORA: Reconstruction is of the Roman period; the oldest classical buildings are in the lower right.

called Athenians, because they lived in the peninsula of Attica, along with about 140 other small villages in Athenian territory.

Such increasingly urban living, with rising populations and new forms of structuring society and territory, brought struggles over borders for land. As borders defined the territories of the growing city-states, the people built forts and shrines to mark them. Legends about the founding of each polis created a community history, reinforced by telling stories and creating shrines for local mythical heroes.

Some city-states had hereditary kings; others were run by a council of elites or elders, which is called an aristocracy. Many cities had some form of both, so that kings needed the consensus of the community leaders to rule.

Corinth had a long line of kings, which even included mythical Bellerophon and his pet winged horse, Pegasus. A very old town, strategically located near the narrow isthmus that separated central from southern Greece, Corinth has been excavated since 1896 by the American School of Classical Studies in Athens. The number of burials there helps us measure population growth, which exploded between the tenth and seventh centuries B.C. The hereditary kings ruled together with an aristocratic council of 200 men until 657 B.C., when Cypselus rose up and made himself its sole leader, called a tyrannos or tyrant.

Between 800 and 500 B.C., the Greeks built more than 1,000 city-states like Corinth, most settled no farther than 25 miles from the coast along the Mediterranean. The most historically significant ones include Athens, with its peninsula Attica; Sparta, which controlled the regions called Laconia, Lacedaemonia, and Messenia; Thebes, which controlled Boeotia; Argos in the Argolid region near Mycenae; and Corinth, which held sway over the area of the Peloponnese closest to central Greece. Think of these as counties inside a state the size of North Carolina, which has just about the same area as Greece.

A polis like Miletus, in Asia Minor, on the west coast of Turkey, had 100,000 people living in it, but most had just 20,000 or so residents. Centuries later, by the beginning of the Peloponnesian War in 432 B.C., Athens became the most populous city-state with at least 150,000 free Athenians, 50,000 resident aliens, and more than 100,000 slaves.

Greeks thought that a self-sufficient, autonomous city-state was an ideal worth fighting for. Much later, Aristotle would say "man is a political animal," by which he meant humans are social creatures, meant for living in a polis.

GOLD AND IVORY STATUE, DELPHI: Ivory head, embossed gold plates, and disks are from an Archaic cult statue.

ON COLONIZATION

THE ORIGINAL FAMILIES who established the city-states in the Iron Age had divided up the land, and as new families joined, they settled on peripheral land. First sons inherited property, but a second or third son had to ask his older brother for permission to continue to live on that land, or claim peripheral land for his own family.

As populations grew, second and third sons became frustrated that they couldn't own good land. At the same time, trade was expanding. Young men heard about fortunes being made abroad. When they visited the great sanctuaries at Delphi or Olympia, they met people from outside Greece, who lived in Sicily or along the Black Sea. The men of Greece were raised hearing stories of adventure in the Age of Heroes. In *The Iliad* and *The Odyssey,* tales familiar to all, travel led to wealth. It was not difficult to find volunteers to found new towns and make their own way in the world.

As a group, the would-be colonists would sail off to the foreign place, often on the advice of Delphi. A famous oracle was given to the

WINE CUP: Two mariners race on a windy sea with sails billowing; found in Etruria, late sixth century B.C.

inhabitants of Santorini, who were suffering from a drought, that told them to found a colony in Libya. It would become Cyrene, a spot where spectacular Greek architecture remains. After hearing this oracle, the ambassadors said, "But we do not even know where to find this Libya of which you speak!" so Delphi provided guides.

Hospitality customs became important as people traveled. There were no hotels, so travelers relied on the kindness of strangers. Homer showed this in *The Iliad* and *The Odyssey:* When visitors arrived, they received food, water, and a bath. Only later would they be asked their name and why they came. Sanctuaries, the sacred grounds around a temple, were safe for everyone. If a man was being chased, he could cling to an altar and not be harmed.

The polis evolved into the metropolis, the mother-city, when founders of new cities brought their home customs and laws with them, as well as a bit of fire from the home city's hearth. The colonists also brought their preferred styles of clothing, worship, music, architecture, pottery, and language. They used the same religious calendar and law codes as the metropolis, at least at first. These colonists spread the Greek influence widely through the ancient world. Greek towns have been

CORINTH: The Archaic Temple of Apollo. Corinth was an early and important metropolis for many colonies.

WHEN MOTHER-CITIES AND THEIR DAUGHTER-CITIES DON'T GET ALONG

THE GREEKS USED FAMILY metaphors to describe colonization. The metropolis is the mother-city. *Apoikia,* the word for "colonies," literally means "the places away from home," because *oikos* is the word for "household." The *oikistes,* "homesteader," was selected from the elite to found a colony. For Syracuse, the founder Archias was from an old Corinthian family, and he had some clout. But he was not in the inner circle of leaders, or why would he leave? Some unfulfilled ambition or resentment must have motivated him. Archias was joined by dissatisfied men with a lust for adventure and a desire to make names for themselves. So why did so many of the apoikia, like Syracuse, become greater than their mother-cities? The colonists were determined to show the metropolis what they could do. That urge to compete is behind the remarkable flowering of Greek civilization in the Archaic age.

excavated in Kerch and at Chersonesus in the Crimean Peninsula, and Batumi on the Black Sea coast of Georgia. Istanbul stands on the site of Byzantium, a Greek colony, which became the new capital of the Roman Empire 1,000 years later. There is a Greek town in Spain, called Gades in ancient times and now called Cadiz. The colony Massalia, which became one of the greatest seaports on the Mediterranean, is now Marseille, France. (Talk about lasting impact: The Ionian colonists brought grapevines to France.) The Greeks who sailed to the Near East founded Cyrene in Libya, Naucratis in Egypt, and Al Mina in Syria. Such a dramatic extension of Greek culture would not be matched until Alexander the Great brought Greek civilization from the Mediterranean to the Middle East.

Although the colonies had cultural ties to their mother-cities, at first there wasn't much trade or communication between them. Those who left had to make it on their own. Sometimes hard feelings caused rifts,

MAP: Most important Greek colonies and their mother-cities in the Mediterranean. More than 1,000 Greek city-states were founded in the Iron Age and Archaic periods.

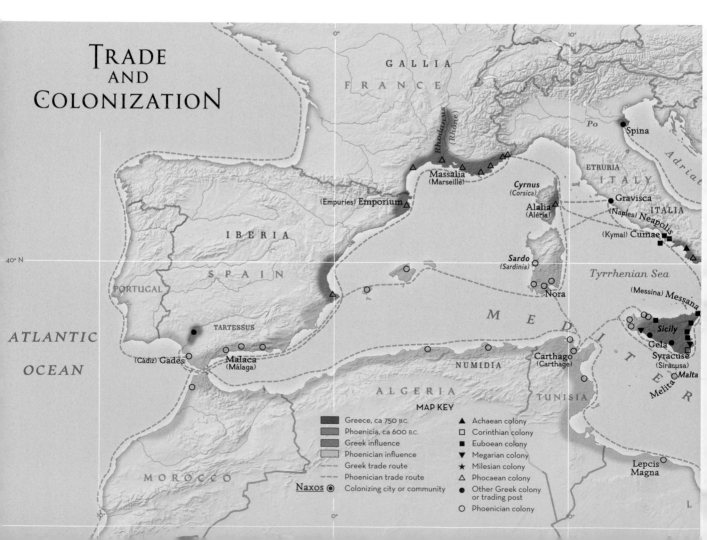

TRADE AND COLONIZATION

GALLIA
FRANCE

Rhodanus (Rhône)

Massalia (Marseille)

Cyrnus (Corsica)

Alalia (Aléria)

Po

Spina

ETRURIA
ITALY

Gravisca

(Naples) Neapolis   ITALIA

(Kymai) Cumae

(Empuries) Emporium

IBERIA

SPAIN

PORTUGAL

TARTESSUS

Sardo (Sardinia)

Nora

Tyrrhenian Sea

(Messina) Messana

Sicily

Gela

Syracuse (Siracusa)

ATLANTIC OCEAN

(Cádiz) Gades

Malaca (Málaga)

NUMIDIA

Carthago (Carthage)

M E D I T E R

Malta

Melita

ALGERIA

TUNISIA

MOROCCO

Lepcis Magna

MAP KEY

■ Greece, ca 750 B.C.	▲ Achaean colony
■ Phoenicia, ca 600 B.C.	□ Corinthian colony
Greek influence	■ Euboean colony
Phoenician influence	▼ Megarian colony
--- Greek trade route	★ Milesian colony
--- Phoenician trade route	△ Phocaean colony
<u>Naxos</u> ◉ Colonizing city or community	● Other Greek colony or trading post
	○ Phoenician colony

based first on the resentments that motivated the younger sons to leave, and then on the lack of support they received once they established their new towns. Over time, some of these newer city-states became powerful, even overshadowing their mother-cities, which increased tension.

One of the early colonizers was Corinth, a powerhouse in the Archaic period whose Temple of Apollo still partially stands. The Corinthians settled Syracuse on Sicily in 734 B.C., according to Thucydides, the fifth-century B.C. historian: "Archias, one of the Heraclidae, came from Corinth and founded Syracuse, first driving the Sicels out from Ortygia," he wrote, "and there the inner city no longer surrounded by the sea still stands; in process of time the outer city was included within the walls and became populous." The land was already occupied by the natives who gave Sicily its name, but the "sons of Hercules"—the Heraclidae, who believed they were descended from the mythical hero—pushed out those earlier inhabitants.

HEROES

GREEK VALUES AND THE GOOD LIFE

I N THE IRON AGE, people lived in such humble circumstances that they would never have had opportunities to test themselves in great wars or live in grand palaces, but the epics of Homer allowed them to imagine such a world. Homer's *Iliad* and *Odyssey* had hundreds of characters, including gods, goddesses, woodland nymphs, and sea creatures, each with their own backstories. At night, professional singer-songwriters visited Greek communities and told tales, sang songs, and explored grand themes of what the good, full life was, and what it meant to be heroic.

Deep within the poetry, drama, philosophy, hymns, and law codes written by the Greeks are some values most of them shared. Most of these were already present in the Iron Age and the following Archaic period, which began in about 750 B.C. How the same values emerged simultaneously across all the isolated villages is mysterious. The traveling bards who sang Homer's epics and made up their own songs may have spread these values like dandelion seeds.

The beliefs developed in the eighth through sixth centuries B.C. contributed to the flowering of Greek culture in the later classical period. The competitive spirit and passion for excellence— what the Greeks called arête—encouraged self-improvement and the rise of individual expression. Although wealth was certainly good, it should be gained fairly and lawfully.

Success in battle or on the racetrack was always thanks to a god or goddess, and offerings were mandatory. Bragging and boasting was vulgar because it gave no credit to the gods, and even Hercules had to muck the Augean stables. Hubris, an overbearing arrogance, was the worst trait and the foundation for Greek tragedies. One must never feel too secure because the wheel of fortune can turn at any moment.

WINE CUP, INTERIOR: Athena, having removed her helmet, serves Hercules a drink after his labors.

Men wanted to be famous, but only when fame was earned for bravery, great deeds, or athletic victories. Fame was different from rumor, which also put your name on people's lips but for the wrong reasons.

Having sons to carry on your work was a good thing, and young men were encouraged to sacrifice themselves for the sake of their elders, on the battlefield or in the family. Strength and endurance were highly valued in men, but it was important to balance the physical with emotional and intellectual strength. Holding one's temper and tongue was a sign of self-control. Avoiding bad feelings, such as anger and distrust and envy, was thought to contribute to a good life. Loyalty to family, community, and city-state was rewarded by good friendships.

Being willing to listen and think about something before acting was important. This contributed to wisdom, and being seen as wise was highly honored. Political decisions needed to be talked through—endlessly, it seems—and learning to weigh factors called for critical thinking skills that led to inquiry in other sectors, too. The Greeks learned to make arguments, defend their positions, and ask questions. They shared a mental openness to trying new ways of doing things, which led to steady innovation in technology and in political institutions.

Generosity, especially giving hospitality graciously without expectation of a return, made good sense, because a visitor might be a god in disguise. Humor was prized, too, and it was good to have a repertoire of witty jokes and stories to entertain friends. These values and points of view are embedded in all ancient Greek literature.

The myths of heroes like Hercules showed the Greeks what could happen if they tried their very best to live a good life. Such legends show that after stumbling blocks and hurdles, barriers and curveballs that have been thrown, soldiering on, outwitting adversaries, and doing the impossible can win immortal fame.

An abiding character trait of the Greeks is a love of life, of living, regardless of status. Consider this chilling scene from Homer's *Odyssey*. Odysseus has stopped at the underworld to ask for directions to get home. He sees many dead friends from the Trojan War. He finds Achilles down there, and reassures him that his reputation on earth is godlike. Achilles is not impressed by this, and says, "Glorious Odysseus: Don't try to reconcile me to my dying. I'd rather serve as another man's laborer, as a poor peasant without land, and be alive on Earth, than be lord of all the lifeless dead."

WEARY HERCULES: Roman interpretation of a famous classical bronze statue by Lysippus, from Perga, Turkey.

ODYSSEUS: This wine bowl depicts Odysseus tied to the mast, his crew's ears plugged with wax, hearing the Sirens' song.

THE ILIAD AND THE ODYSSEY

THE ILIAD IS A WAR STORY. Its heroes embrace a code of valor that the Archaic Greeks emulated. It took nearly ten years for the Greeks to win, using the ruse of the Trojan horse to get men inside the walls. The elite took on characteristics and ethics of the heroes they admired in Homer. Being brave, noble, self-sacrificing, strong, clever, healthy, good-looking, and warlike was all bundled into what the Greeks called *agathos*.

Homer's *Odyssey* shows the hero after the fall of Troy. He leads his men back to Greece, but it takes another ten years, and Odysseus is the only one who makes it home alive. He visits many places, cursed and helped along the way by Poseidon and Athena, facing challenges with bravery and ingenuity. At the same time, *The Odyssey* is a story of his son coming of age. Telemachus was too young to remember his father, and wants to hear stories and get to know the man by interviewing other Greek heroes who returned home. He sets out to find out what happened to Odysseus so that he and his mother, Penelope, can either keep waiting or move on. Additionally, the tale is a love story between Odysseus and Penelope, focused not on falling in love, but on staying in love, and learning to trust each other after the 20-year absence. Penelope's warrior husband left her to fight the Trojan War, not knowing he would be gone so long. Penelope was the hero's true north, and their reunion shows they were equal partners in the marriage.

MYKONOS VASE: *(opposite)* The earliest depiction of the Trojan horse in Greek art, this storage jar dates to 670 B.C.

WHY ARE THE GREEK MALE STATUES NAKED?

YOUNG GREEK MEN spent their days in the palaestra, taking lessons and training in athletics—in the raw. If somebody spent that much time working out, then it was likely that he was also well educated in literature, mathematics, and music. In Greek culture, men admired each other's looks and had no reservations expressing that to each other. They made bronze and marble male nude statues, called kouroi, to mark graves of good men. On temples, battles show naked heroes—sometimes they wear sandals and a cape but nothing else—fighting clothed adversaries. This suggests that the nudity is "heroic."

KOUROS

FROM CITIZENS TO SOLDIERS

I N EVERY GREEK CITY-STATE, the male citizen-farmer-soldiers were the backbones. Armies varied in size and training, but from place to place soldiers dressed the same, had the same arms and armor, and shared a code of ethics. Between 725 and 650 B.C. foot soldiers became known as hoplites. They fought shoulder to shoulder in a dense formation called a phalanx, usually eight rows deep. Battles didn't start until both sides were ready. Surprise attacks or night attacks were considered uncivilized. There were times when Greeks agreed not to fight, such as the height of harvest or dead of winter. Truces were called for the Olympic Games, so athletes and spectators could travel safely. In other words, Greek warfare was full of gentlemanly agreements, like our Geneva Conventions, and violators were considered un-Greek.

DISCUS THROWER: Muscular athlete in a classical moment, just before his throw, on an Athenian prize amphora

Hoplite uniforms included a cotton tunic (called a chiton) with a pleated skirt; a leather and bronze breastplate; greaves, which are bronze versions of the shin guards soccer players wear today; and helmets with horsehair crests. Their weapons included a spear, a sword, and a round shield.

Greeks fought proudly, as it tested their courage, like the heroes of the Trojan War. This marching song captures the spirit, from a Cretan poet named Hybrias of the sixth century B.C.; he says that even though he is a farmer, when he puts on his arms as a soldier, he feels like a superhero: "I have great wealth: a spear and a sword and a fine leather shield to protect my skin. For with this I plough, with this I reap, with this I trample the sweet wine from the vines, with this I am called master of serfs. Those who do not dare to have a spear and a sword and a fine leather shield to protect their skin all cower at my knee and prostrate themselves, calling me master and great king."

When these men faced life-or-death situations together, they came to depend upon and respect each other in civic life. When hoplites went to battle, the phalanx marched in time. Each man held his spear up in his right hand and his large round shield up in his left. That meant the fellow to his left had coverage from that round shield as well, leaving his spear-throwing arm protected but free.

The raised shields made a defensive wall of bronze. Say the enemy launched arrows. The whole row of men lifted their shields at a 45-degree angle, as did all the rows behind them. If they were lucky, the arrows bounced off. But all must act as one.

Shields were not only important, but also expensive. One poem from the early seventh century B.C. described shameful behavior that would make good citizen-soldiers shake their heads and roll their eyes: "Some barbarian is waving my shield, since I was obliged to leave that perfectly good piece of equipment under a bush. But I got away, so what does it matter? Let the shield go; I can buy another one equally good." This seems to be the opposite of hoplite values, yet somehow it was repeated orally and then survived in written form for more than 2,700 years—perhaps because listeners felt superior to the selfish coward.

NIKE, THE GODDESS OF VICTORY

NIKE OF
SAMOTHRACE

THE GREEKS PRAYED FOR victory before each battle. They imagined that Nike, the goddess of victory, circled the battlefield like a blimp at a football game. When her toe touched the ground, the army on that side of the battlefield would win. Praying to her before battle was just common sense, and the Greeks built many victory monuments to her at sanctuaries in thanks for her support.

The pose of Nike in the "Winged Victory of Samothrace" depicts the moment when Nike landed on a ship, granting victory in a naval battle. Her drapery swirls like the fog of war, still in motion from flying in the wind, the forces pressing her dress against her chest. Victory feels great, and the ancient artist knew how to make us desire her.

THE OLYMPIC GAMES

Tʜᴇ ᴛʀᴀᴅɪᴛɪᴏɴ ᴏғ funeral games went back to the Age of Heroes, according to Homer, with contests honoring the deceased and a feast afterward. Athletes dedicated their performance to the god whose festival they were attending. At the Olympics, it was the great god Zeus.

Legends say that in 776 ʙ.ᴄ., the first games at Olympia were funeral games for a local king, whose son-in-law, Pelops, organized the tribute. (The Peloponnesus was named for him. *Nessos* comes from the Greek word for "island," so southern Greece is Pelops's island—almost true except for the isthmus at Corinth that connects it to the mainland.)

Another legend says Hercules established the games at the place where Pelops was buried. The site is in far western Peloponnesus, not exactly convenient for Greeks to reach from elsewhere. Weeks before the festival, heralds announced a sacred truce during which all conflicts ceased so athletes, trainers, and the public could travel safely.

People from all over the Mediterranean arrived daily, pitching tents and camping for about a month. Like at a huge tailgate party, they would share food, buy souvenirs, and tell stories until the main contests began. Of course there were processions and festival activities before and after the events. One highlight was the opening ceremony, with a procession around the sanctuary's 72 altars.

ᴏʟʏᴍᴘɪᴄ ᴀᴛʜʟᴇᴛᴇ: A champion at Olympia wins an olive wreath in closing ceremony.

The games included wrestling, boxing, running, discus, javelin, long jump, chariot racing, and more. No older culture had any of these track-and-field sports with the exception of racing. The length of the race was called a *stade,* so the place where runners race that length became a stadium.

As with the modern triathlon, men could compete in a combination of sports. The pentathlon combined wrestling, racing, javelin throw, discus, and the long jump on a single day. The *pankration* was the most

THE STATUE OF ZEUS: ONE OF THE SEVEN WONDERS OF THE ANCIENT WORLD

PHIDIAS, SCULPTOR OF THE STATUE of Athena inside the Parthenon, came to Olympia in the third quarter of the fifth century B.C. He built a hangar to work on his statue at the same scale as the inside of the great temple there. His finished gold-and-ivory figure was about 40 feet tall, depicting Zeus on his throne atop an ornate podium. People fainted and swooned when they saw it, as if they had seen the god himself. Some said their lives had been changed. Pilgrims came to Olympia just to worship Zeus, even without the games going on. Later, Greeks and then Romans visited Olympia to see the statue, which writers dubbed one of the Seven Wonders of the Ancient World. It still remained intact in A.D. 394 at the time of the 293rd Olympiad, when the Roman Emperor Theodosius I proclaimed all pagan sanctuaries closed, and the Olympics ended. The statue was transported to Constantinople (now Istanbul) where it was destroyed in a fire in A.D. 475, at 900 years old.

STATUE OF OLYMPIAN ZEUS

brutal combination. Men boxed and wrestled, with barely any rules, much like modern mixed-martial arts.

Champions became legendary. For example, Milo of Croton, from southern Italy, won six wreaths in wrestling. His conditioning system was brilliant: He put a baby calf on his shoulders and carried the animal around, each day picking him up and carrying him some more. As the calf gained weight, Milo was able to handle it. In a year, he was carrying around a cow. This made wrestling a human much easier.

A successful Olympic athlete would receive his wreath at a public ceremony. From his town, he would get free meals and the best seats in theaters for life. He could pay to set up a monument in the sanctuary. Poets wrote poems and sang songs about the victor and his race so the folks back home could hear about it. Pindar, the most famous of those poets, wrote this for a victor: "Strike up, then, the thrum of the lyre, lift up the flute's cry . . . I will work out for that hero praise that shall ring far."

OLIVE OIL PRIZE: A champion of a foot race in Athens won this oil-filled amphora.

OLYMPIA

UNIQUE AND WONDERFUL places inspired the Greeks, who built temples and sanctuaries there. They liked to put temples on hilltops, promontories, overlooks, or places with Cyclopean stones peeking out. At first Olympia seems not to fit the pattern. It is flat, lacking the dramatic landscapes of Delphi or Pergamon.

Olympia, however, sits at the meeting of two rivers, depicted as river gods on the pediments of the Temple of Olympian Zeus. It is lush and green, even in the height of summer. There are wildflowers beyond count in the spring. Olympia even feels and sounds different from other places. It is always cooler, and there are so many birds and cicadas that you can hardly hear yourself speak. Because the trees are all over and the ground is flat, it is difficult to get a view of the whole site—the sanctuary appears to just keep going and going, blessed by the gods and preserved by mortals as a sacred spot.

ATHLETICS

OLYMPIA WASN'T THE ONLY game around. A circuit of four Panhellenic games, one per year, rotated from Olympia's sanctuary to Zeus, to Delphi's Pythian Apollo, to Nemea's sanctuary in honor of Zeus, and to Isthmia where Poseidon was worshipped. That is why the Olympics come once every four years.

The only prizes the athletes received on the podium were the wreaths, which don't seem all that valuable to us—olive branches were given at Olympia, laurel at Delphi, pine at Isthmia, and parsley at Nemea. (Yes, that is correct—parsley.) Their home cities rewarded the winners handsomely, however. A decree found in Athens set the prize money for a victorious athlete at the Olympics at 500 drachmas, which was a fortune. Champions at Isthmia would get 100 drachmas. They also got a pension plan, with free meals for life.

Were athletics just for men? Ancient literature shows that women played ball, juggled hoops, danced, swam, hunted, rode horses, drove chariots, and of course ran footraces.

Women were not allowed to see the competitions at the Olympics. Because they kept sneaking in, though, a law decreed that any woman caught would get a death sentence. It seems that was an empty threat and was never carried out, so far as we know. One mother wanted to watch her son compete, so she disguised herself as a trainer. She was found out, and from then on, trainers had to strip naked before they were allowed to coach their athletes.

Why were they so strict about keeping women out? Perhaps it was about modesty and virtue, but more likely the men wanted to have a good time without their wives. Married women were excluded from the campgrounds, but sex workers and unmarried girls were permitted, and perhaps encouraged. During the games these women would wait in the campground. A proper hotel opened in the fourth century B.C. to accommodate rich people, but the vast majority of fans slept outside.

At another time of the year, a festival with games just for women was held at Olympia in honor of Hera, Zeus's wife. A committee of 16 women organized the competitions. Young unmarried women competed for prizes in the footraces. A second-century A.D. Roman author described the single-strap uniforms the runners

DISCUS THROWER: A Greek original bronze known as Myron's "Discobolus" inspired this Roman marble statue.

RUNNERS: The length of a race was called a stade, so the place they raced in was called a stadium.

wore: "Their hair hangs down, a tunic reaches to a little above the knee, and they bare the right shoulder as far as the breast." Leaving their long hair down seems a little odd, not only because most women today would likely tie their hair back while working out, but also because Greek girls customarily wore a single braid.

Because the competitors at the festival for Hera at Olympia represented their cities, it suggests that there must have been tryouts. For these athletes to be fit to compete, they must have had training and workouts. We must conclude that some women in ancient Greece exercised and even became good enough to compete nationally.

Be it funeral games, dramatic contests, religious festival games, or war, there were winners and losers. The word for "contest" in Greek is *agon,* and our word "agony" comes from it. Winners could strut their stuff as they were crowned with wreaths before the crowds and then they could set up victory monuments or trophies. Olympia and Delphi were full of them. What remains today are usually just the bases, often inscribed with an epigram or statement of who won. The bronze statues, tripods, or sphinxes that were on top are gone, looted by Hellenistic kings, or Roman soldiers, or removed and taken to modern museums.

CHARIOT: The four-horse chariot race was the most prestigious event at the Olympics.

HOW DID THEY HIT THE SHOWERS IN ANCIENT GREECE?

ATHLETE'S EQUIPMENT

BEFORE WORKING OUT or competing, Greek athletes rubbed their bodies with olive oil, which they carried in a small clay bottle. They exercised in the raw, so the oil went everywhere. Then, like gymnasts use chalk on their hands to get a grip, the men applied a fine coat of sand. Everywhere! Supposedly the sand worked as a sunblock, too. After the event, the athletes used a sponge and a strigil, a kind of scraper, to clean up. The bronze strigil is shaped like celery bent into a question mark. An athlete held the straight end and scraped his body. The gunk and dirt went into the trough. The strigil removed most sand, then the man used the sponge to reach those parts the strigil might hurt. Some men were buried with their strigil, just in case they needed to compete in the afterlife.

MILITARY CONTESTS

THE HEROES THESEUS AND HERCULES were not gods, exactly, but mortals with semidivine parents. The heroes had close relationships with gods and goddesses who guided and tested them. They represented life, with its continuous trials that paid off in the end.

Hercules fought battles and performed his 12 labors mostly near Mycenae, in the area we associate with the Spartan allies. Classical Greeks visited these places to stand where the great hero once triumphed.

Theseus was the model of a brave warrior and wise leader. He was also an early king of Athens, so most myths have him founding Athenian traditions or saving the city-state in some way. He unified the tiny villages in Attica, with Athens as their common civic center.

War was the ultimate contest, and every time the Greeks went into battle, images of their heroes filled their heads. The Age of Heroes would have been the Age of Average Joes if it weren't for the Trojan War, which immortalized these men through the stories told of them.

In the seventh century B.C. the Spartans expanded to conquer the people of adjacent Messenia, and then to take over about a third of the Peloponnesus. When they won, they enslaved the losers. These people, called helots, remained enslaved for centuries, doing all the work so the Spartans could train as professional warriors. Helots vastly outnumbered the Spartan citizens, resulting in constant tension and fear, and ever harsher controls over the enslaved population.

In the sixth century, cities fought, as did factions inside cities. Sometimes two nobles would want to lead at the same time, and they would get armed gangs together to fight it out. When they won, the Greeks called them tyrants.

This civil unrest is a form of heroic contest, too. In Athens, a tyrant named Peisistratus sought power. In one attempt, he drove into town in a chariot, with a tall blonde dressed as Athena behind him, to give the impression that he was her choice. It didn't work. Another time, he

PARTHENON METOPE: Mythical battles between centaurs and Lapiths show noble men fighting against their bestial nature.

beat himself up and asked for bodyguards. The council assigned him some, who then went around beating up his rivals. It took armed conflict to achieve his goal. He and his sons ruled Athens from 546 to 510 B.C.

The two most significant conflicts in Greece in the fifth century B.C. were the Persian War and the Peloponnesian War. The Persian War was between the Greeks and invaders with an entirely different culture. The kings of the Persian Empire in the early fifth century had grand palaces in Iraq and Iran, and dominated the vast area from the coasts of Turkey, Syria, Lebanon, Israel, and Egypt to the border of Afghanistan and Pakistan. They conquered the Greek city-states in Ionia, along the west coast of Turkey, and imposed harsh rules and taxes. The war between the Greeks and Persians from 490 to 479 B.C. was a contest for the survival of Greek independence, and with that, their way of life.

The Peloponnesian War was different. Both sides were Greek—the Spartans and their allies against the Athenians and their allies. All the cities backed one or the other, so for the Greek world, it was cataclysmic. The war had two phases, 431–421 B.C., which ended in a draw, and 413–404 B.C., when Sparta beat Athens. One catastrophic decision the Athenians made was to send 200 ships and men to support a civil war on Sicily in 415 B.C. They didn't know the territory, the promised funds were a fiction, their generals were incompetent, and the whole island was hostile to them. Most of the men were killed or taken prisoner and sold as slaves. When the war with Sparta heated up in 413 B.C., Athens was in no shape to put up a good fight. In 404 B.C., Sparta won.

The war's end by no means meant the end of conflict. First Sparta overreached, installing military bases inside Greek cities and tearing down their defensive walls. This made them unpopular victors, so many of the cities allied with Thebes against the Spartans. The men of Thebes beat the Spartans at Leuctra in 371 B.C., and then the Thebans basically turned around and did the same thing—installing military bases and intimidating cities. In the Battle of Mantinea in 362 B.C., Sparta and Thebes lost too many men on both sides and called it a tie. At this time, Macedonia was expanding under Alexander the Great's father, Philip II. By 338 B.C. Macedonia had conquered all the Greeks.

THESEUS AND MINOTAUR: Wine cup interior showing Knossos and labyrinth in center, surrounded by the six labors of Theseus

AMONS

IN MYTHOLOGY, HERCULES, Theseus, and Achilles met and even married wild warrior women who fought on horseback. They were said to have come from Scythia, north and west of the Black Sea. Homer and Herodotus mention these women, called Amazons, and tell of their encounters with the Greeks.

Alexander the Great is said to have received an embassy of Amazons who visited him when he was near Tehran in 330 B.C. The Amazon queen insisted he get her pregnant and stayed six weeks. Satisfied the deed was done, the women rode off.

Most scholars regarded these stories as myths until archaeological excavations on the border between Russia and Kazakhstan in the 1990s revealed 150 graves of women with legs bowed from riding, buried with armor. And DNA tests on bones in warrior graves in the steppes around the Black Sea show that 20 to 30 percent were female, buried with arms and weapons, not jewelry and perfume bottles.

THE TRAGEDY OF AJAX: WHAT IT MEANT TO BE SECOND BEST

AJAX AND ACHILLES: Two warriors play dice between battles; amphora by Exekias, mid-sixth century B.C.

AJAX CARRIES ACHILLES: Ajax takes Achilles off the battlefield at Troy; detail from the François Vase.

A POPULAR GREEK DRINKING SONG spells out how doubly painful it can be first to be compared to your father, and then after superseding him, be bested by a peer. As the anonymous author wrote, "Ajax of the ponderous spear, mighty son of Telamon, they call you bravest of the Greeks, next to the great Achilles. Telamon came first, and of the Greeks the second man was Ajax, and with him there came invincible Achilles."

As athletes, many of us would be happy to come in second. Coming in fourth would upset us, not being on the podium or medaling. But in ancient Greece, it was come in first, or not at all.

Sophocles told the story of Ajax as a Greek tragedy, but 100 years before he wrote the play, the legend appeared painted on ceramics and was widely known. On many decorated clay amphorae, the double-handled liquid containers, we see two soldiers playing dice. Their arms are nearby, ready at a moment's notice. They are Odysseus and Ajax, and in very tiny letters coming out of their mouths, Odysseus says "four" while Ajax says "three," so Ajax is losing. The artist has selected a moment in time just before battle. The battle they wait for is a peak moment in the Trojan War, because Achilles died, struck in the heel. Mighty Ajax picked up the body of Achilles and carried him off the battlefield. At his funeral, the soldiers debated over who should be awarded Achilles' armor. It came down to two men, both heroes but for different reasons: Odysseus, whose cunning, intelligence, and leadership skills were so admired, and Ajax, a tall, strong fellow, arguably the best in combat of all the Greeks. The men voted, and Ajax came in second. Shortly thereafter, he killed himself.

Homer lets us visit Ajax in the underworld. Odysseus descends and sees the heroes who died in the Trojan War. Of course, losing to Odysseus was the reason Ajax killed himself. Odysseus wants to make peace with him, and calls him over. Here is the scene as Homer presents it in *The Odyssey:*

"The other ghosts of the dead departed stood there sorrowing, and each asked me about their dear ones. Only the spirit of Ajax, Telamon's son, stood apart, still angered over my victory in the contest by the ships, for Achilles' weapons. Achilles' divine mother, Thetis, had offered them as a prize, with the Trojan prisoners and Pallas Athene herself as judges. I wish I had never won the reward for that debate, that armor that caused the earth to close over so noble a head as that of Ajax, who in beauty and martial action was supreme among the Danaans, save for that faultless son of Peleus. I spoke to his ghost in calming words: 'Ajax, son of faultless Telamon, even in death can you not forget your anger with me, over those fatal weapons? The gods themselves must have cursed the Argives with them. In you a tower of strength was lost to us, and we Achaeans never cease to share as great a grief for you, as we do for Achilles, Peleus's son. But Zeus alone is to blame whose deadly hatred for the Danaan host [Mycenaeans] hastened your doom. Come closer to me, my lord, so you can hear my speech. Curb your wrath: restrain your proud spirit.' He chose not to give a single word in answer, but went his way into Erebus to join the other ghosts of the dead departed."

A carving on the base of a statue in the Athenian cemetery, dated to 540 B.C., says, "Stand and mourn for me, Croisos, whom raging Ares destroyed one day, fighting in the front line." His family wanted it known that he was killed in the line of duty for his city. They blame the god of war, Ares. Of course, Ares also killed Achilles, and something like post traumatic stress took the life of Ajax.

THE COMPETITIVE SPIRIT IN DEATH

HOCKEY PLAYERS

AN ANCIENT GREEK cemetery was like a gallery of handsome men and beautiful women, frozen in stone. In the late sixth century B.C. a remarkable statue base (see p. 95) depicted two old men, seated, with a cat and a dog on leashes. Yes, a cat on a leash—not so effective for walking, but perhaps good for a cat fight. The dog and the cat are about to tussle, as the men watch. Even old men, beyond their years of competing in athletics, wanted to express their competitive spirit, and found ways to do so through their surrogates, the animals. Other scenes carved on statue bases show two boys playing what looks like hockey, fighting for a puck; some depict them playing ball and showing off their perfect physiques, or wrestling, while a coach taps them with a stick to correct their stance or position. Greeks competed even after death for how handsome they were as well as how athletic.

INTELLECTUAL CURIOSITY

THE ARCHAIC AGE SAW the rise of a group of intellectuals who shared ideas, taught, traveled, gave advice, and wrote down their thoughts. Heraclitus of Ephesus coined a term for them, "philosophers." *Philo* means "lover," and *sophia* means "wisdom," so they were wisdom-lovers. There is no literature like theirs from earlier or contemporary civilizations. These men enjoyed puzzles, and many mind games have been passed down to our day. Perhaps this one sounds familiar: "What is the one thing on earth that is two-legged, and

LYRE PLAYER: Reposing banqueter with lyre; fresco on a wall of the Tomb of the Diver, Paestum.

three-legged, and four-legged, but goes by only one name; and uniquely, of all creatures that crawl, swim, or fly on earth, is capable of changing its very nature; and the more legs he uses, the slower he moves?" This is the riddle of the Sphinx, which Oedipus cleverly answered as "man." The philosophers also wrote paradoxes, which trained their students to think critically and systematically. Try Zeno's paradox, paraphrased by Aristotle: "If everything when it occupies an equal space is at rest, and if that which is in locomotion is always occupying such a space at any moment, the flying arrow is therefore motionless."

Some of these intellectuals made observations with lasting impact to math and science, including Pythagoras and Democritus.

Pythagoras formed the Pythagorean theorem about the sides of triangles, still taught today. Traveling exposed him to ideas that fed his mind. Born on the island Samos in about 570 B.C., he visited the philosopher Thales in Miletus as a youth, then traveled to Tyre in Lebanon, and to Egypt, too. He spent time in Babylon where he studied with the magi (Persian wise men) and learned Babylonian astronomy and mathematics. Later in life he founded a philosophical school in Sicily. He saw patterns in numbers and symbols, and believed that reality had a mathematical core and that the universe can be reduced to a scale and a number.

ATALANTA, TEGEA: The goddess Atalanta, a marble architectural sculpture from Athena Alea Temple

Democritus lived a bit later, joining the conversation after many philosophers had debated whether water, air, fire, or something else altogether was the building block for everything on Earth. Democritus proposed that the common element in everything was the atom. In Greek the word *tomein* means "to cut in half," and the "a" is a negative like our "un," so the *a-toma* literally means "the unsplittable thing." Of course, he never imagined the atomic bomb, but his idea was a foundation.

Abstract thinking such as this about the universe put human life in perspective. A poem by Leonidas captures the lofty peaks from which philosophers looked down on humankind: "O man, infinite was the time before you came to light, and infinite will be the time to come in Hades. The portion of life that remains for you is but a pin-prick, or whatever is tinier than a pin-prick. Yours is a micro-life, sorrowful, but even that is not sweet but more hateful than your enemy, death . . . Ask yourself at the dawn of every day, O man, what your strength is and learn to lie low, content with a simple life; ever remembering in your heart, as long as you dwell among the living, from what pieces of straw you are held together."

THE GREEK CITIES IN ASIA MINOR: HOME OF PHILOSOPHY

I N THE ARCHAIC PERIOD, beautiful Greek colonies were built in Turkey. Richer than the city-states that founded them, the Greeks in this zone are known as Ionians, descended in myth from Ion, as were the Athenians. The cities were close to a major road running along the Turkish coast, and they all had ports where Phoenician sailors from Lebanon docked, so information and new ideas flowed easily.

The Greeks were insatiably curious, and the first to write about their questions and findings. The earliest philosophers lived in Ionia, in Miletus, and in nearby Ephesus. The Maeander River there twists and turns, and silting changed it constantly. Perhaps the earliest philosophers were curious about this. The first philosopher, Thales of Miletus, proposed that all matter is based on water. Heraclitus of Ephesus said you can never step in the same river twice, and declared "all is in flux."

In the early sixth century B.C. Thales asked, what are the fundamental building blocks of the world? From this point, Ionian philosophers proposed various answers. Was water the cosmic principle? Fire? Air? Or a combination? We call the Ionian thinkers the pre-Socratic philosophers in hindsight; they are the intellectuals who came before Socrates. The pre-Socratics put a premium on originality, on bettering what came before, on experimentation, and on unconventional thinking. Miletus's intellectual history was cut short, though: In 494 B.C., the Persians sacked the town for instigating the Ionian Revolt, and as punishment sold the women into slavery and transplanted the men to Iran.

PORTRAITS OF PHILOSOPHERS: No Greek philosophers actually sat for a portrait, so these are based on posthumous verbal descriptions.

The birthplace of Greek philosophy is also where the European use of coins started. Coinage as we know it was first introduced to Europe from Asia Minor. In the seventh century B.C., Lydia controlled most of western Turkey. Nearby Miletus and Ephesus began to use the metal Lydian currency with their colonies, and it spread from there. Each city-state made the currency its own by stamping icons on it. Recurring themes on Greek coins are images of birds, animals, chariots, the profiles of kings (later on), and the gods and goddesses who protected cities.

KARYSTUS, TURKEY
The rooster and the K represent the town
of Karystus; mid-fifth century B.C.

KNOSSOS, CRETE
This first century B.C. labyrinth
symbolizes Knossos.

CATANIA, SICILY
Athena Nike holds victory wreath.
Silver tetradrachm, 465 B.C.

CATANIA, SICILY
River god shown as a kneeling
man-headed bull with tuna below, bird
above. Silver tetradrachm, 465 B.C.

TARENTUM, ITALY
Town celebrates its founder Taras
with a spear on horseback. Silver
stater, late fourth century B.C.

SALAMIS, GREECE
Left obverse, Nike on prow of ship;
right reverse, Poseidon aims his trident.
Silver tetradrachm, 300 B.C.

LAMPSACUS, TURKEY
Left obverse, portrait of King Lysimachus with
horns of Hercules, styled after Alexander;
right reverse, Athena sits with Nike in her
hand. Silver tetradrachm, 300 B.C.

THE GREEK GODS

FOR EVERY HUMAN EMOTION, there is a Greek myth that captures its essence. Think of the first few days of falling in love. One day you feel perfectly fine, the next day you are acting crazy, your heart is racing, and you are writing your two names together in a diary. That is Aphrodite and her adorable, irresistible son, Eros, better known by their Latin names as Venus and Cupid. He has just shot an arrow into your rear when you least expected it.

Feeling tipsy? That is Dionysus taking over your body. (Hey, about last night, he did it, not me!) Have you ever felt the panic of losing a child in a department store? Demeter lost Persephone in a meadow, and the worst possible thing did happen. The Lord of Death, Hades himself, kidnapped her daughter, and raced in his chariot to his underworld palace where he made her his bride. Demeter caused the first winter on Earth in her grief. Or there's Hera, who lived with her lying, cheating, philandering sack of a brother-husband, Zeus, with his 12 lovers (but who's counting?). She fried one girl to a crisp, made another into a crane, and yet another she transformed into a white heifer, forever tortured by a gadfly. Maybe you have felt betrayed by a spouse, consumed with jealous rage and the desire to commit a felony. Medea has been there. Jason left her for a young princess, so Medea murdered the girl and also killed her own two children, who Jason loved more than anything, just to spite him.

Take your pick; there's a myth for every high and low emotional state that deviates from your everyday, normal self.

Greek mythology is not for children. It has to be sanitized pretty thoroughly, and even then, real "morals to the story" are rare, and modern writers feel they have to insert them or bend the originals to provide endings that satisfy modern taste. The Greek gods commit all sorts of sins we can barely talk about. Lying, cheating, and stealing don't even make the top ten list. A goddess castrates her husband. Gods

MOURNING ATHENA: Marble plaque found on the Athenian Acropolis; early fifth century B.C.

repeatedly commit incest and rape. They torture each other and mortals, too. The gods take young girls and boys whenever they please and have their way with them, even if it burns the youths alive. They devour their pregnant lovers, eat their children, and cook other men's sons to serve to their enemies. Goddesses become jealous of mortal women and kill them or turn them into insects and animals. There's plenty of adultery, followed by traps to expose and humiliate the unfaithful spouses.

Sometimes the myths teach direct lessons, for example, warning young people not to drive too aggressively, as we learn from the story of Daedalus the craftsman and his son Icarus, who took the keys to his father's newfangled wings-made-of-wax-and-feathers-mobile, and flew too close to the sun, only to plummet fatally to earth.

Sometimes myths explain the origins of something. Aphrodite (Venus) and Ares (Mars) became lovers, then were caught by Aphrodite's husband, Hephaestus the metalsmith. He devised a bedspread made of chains, and when the lovers laid down, he lifted the four corners and hoisted them up high, like being caught in a fishing net, so that the other gods could point at them and laugh. That explains why we see the planets Mars and Venus together in the night sky; we still point and smile when we notice them. And while we're looking, be sure to spot the Milky Way. Did you know that Hera was nursing baby Hercules, and he had been sucking so hard that he popped off her breast and her milk spurted up to the sky?

BIRTH OF ATHENA: A tiny Athena overlaps the decorative band as she is born from the head of a frontal-facing, seated Zeus.

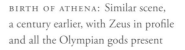

BIRTH OF ATHENA: Similar scene, a century earlier, with Zeus in profile and all the Olympian gods present

A GODDESS IS BORN

EACH MYTH ABOUT A GOD or goddess tells us something about his or her true nature. For instance, contrast the myths about the births of two goddesses, Athena and Aphrodite, who couldn't be more different from each other.

Where do creativity, ingenuity, and decision-making come from? The myth of Athena's birth demonstrates. Zeus and Hera were the ultimate power couple, but Zeus enjoyed many extramarital affairs. His first was with Metis (meaning "deep thought"). She became pregnant. Earth and Heaven warned Zeus that if Metis gave birth, the child would exceed him in wisdom. So Zeus swallowed Metis whole. This had the advantage of keeping her hidden from Hera, too. After nine months, he had a terrible headache. He called the craftsman god Hephaestus to split his head open with an axe to relieve the pressure. Out popped Athena, fully grown, armed and ready.

What does this myth show? When we need inspiration, we need time to digest the problem. Then after a few bad nights and some splitting headaches, we wake up one day and in a moment of inspiration, the full plan is revealed to us. Armed and ready, we know exactly what we must do. Today we represent insight with the lightbulb, but isn't the Greek myth of Athena more accurate and descriptive?

Athena's creation myth reflected her cerebral nature. The story of the birth of Aphrodite, the volatile goddess of love, was anything but intellectual. It all started with a fight about sex between Earth and her husband Heaven. She asked for a volunteer to castrate him, and her youngest son, Cronus, agreed. The poet Hesiod described what happened next:

> And Heaven came, bringing on night and longing for love, and he lay about Earth spreading himself full upon her. Then the son from his ambush stretched forth his left hand and in his right took the great long sickle with jagged teeth, and swiftly lopped off his own father's members and cast them away to fall behind him. And so soon as he had cut off the members with flint and cast them from the land into the surging sea, they were swept away over the main a long time: and a white foam spread around them from the immortal flesh, and in it there grew a maiden . . . She came to sea-girt Cyprus, and came forth an awful and lovely goddess, and grass grew up about her beneath her shapely feet. Gods and men call her Aphrodite, the foam-born goddess.

THE BIRTH OF VENUS: *(opposite)* Aphrodite arrives on Cyprus in the foamy sea. Botticelli's famous painting is inspired by Hesiod's *Theogony.*

GREEK RELIGION AND THE IMMORAL IMMORTALS

HOW CAN PEOPLE WORSHIP these vindictive, jealous, lusty, immoral gods? The relationship between worship of the gods and the myths about them is complicated. Ultimately, though, those stories provided the Greeks with guidance and ways to understand the world.

First consider Athena, goddess of courage and inspiration. Given that everyone becomes religious in a foxhole, when people are desperate for a solution, praying to Athena makes sense. But that is not the only role Athena plays. She is also the goddess of craftsmen and artists. To be successful, craftsmen and artists always need new ideas. Just as the early poets prayed to the Muses, the craftsmen prayed to Athena for the creative inspiration they needed to keep making their products. The citizens of Athens chose Athena over Poseidon to be their patron deity. Why? Athens valued innovation and would need many new ideas and inspiration to develop democracy from scratch. Time after time, the decisions Athenians made were novel and ingenious. Athena is the goddess to call upon when you need to think outside the box.

Hera was worshipped by people who wanted to protect their families, who wanted their no-good husbands to come home, or who wanted revenge on enemies. By extension, she protects the wider family of the city-state. She is the grandmother no one really wants to hang out with, but everyone respects and appreciates as the matriarch. Residents of a city protected by Hera knew no one would mess around with her—or with them.

Artemis and Apollo were twins, born on the island of Delos where their mother, a lover of Zeus, hid during her pregnancy. Both twins were expert shots with the bow and arrow. Artemis lived in the woods, not in cities, preferring moonlight to broad daylight. She protected young girls, shooting boys who came too close to them. Apollo had less

PARTHENON FRIEZE, DETAIL: Poseidon, Apollo, and Artemis from the assembly of the gods; British Museum.

of a trigger finger. He corrected people when they made mistakes, rather than shooting them. He represents civilized city life, complementing his wilder sister. After he took the lyre from Hercules, he became patron of the arts. In life, it is often hard for humans to know what the right thing to do is, because we cannot see into the future. Apollo can. He was the god of the oracle at Delphi. Praying to Apollo for foresight was a way for humans to get help imagining future consequences so they could make decisions.

And then there is Aphrodite. Just about everyone, even in modern times, has prayed to her. A beautiful myth inspired by Aphrodite shows the depth and fleetingness of human love. Achilles, the Bronze Age hero, and his men are attacked by women on horse, the Amazons who were allies of their enemy Troy. The men, on foot, are at a disadvantage, but they fight back. There are casualties on both sides. Achilles finds himself in a duel with Penthesilea, the Amazon queen. He drags her off her horse; she falls to the ground. Achilles puts his sword to her neck, and their eyes meet. Her eyes do not ask for mercy. Her eyes say, "I am falling in love with you." As he gazes at her face, Achilles falls in love with her, in return. But it is too late. His sword has already sliced her jugular.

KORE FROM CHIOS: Found on the Athenian Acropolis, this marble statue was a gift to Athena.

ARES AND
APHRODITE

IN THE BEGINNING, THE GREEK VERSION

HESIOD'S LONG POEM, *Theogony,* or birth of the gods, tells the story of the origins of the universe and how the gods interrelate. He begins with Chaos. "Verily at the first Chaos came to be, but next wide-bosomed Earth (Gaia), the ever sure foundations of all immortals who hold the peaks of snowy Olympus, and dim Tartarus in the depth of wide Earth, and Eros (Love), fairest among the gods, who unnerves the limbs and overcomes the mind and wise counsels of all gods and all men within them. From Chaos came forth Erebus and black Night; but of Night were born Aether and Day, whom she conceived and bore from union in love with Erebus. And Earth first bore starry Heaven, equal to herself, to cover her on every side, and to be an ever-sure dwelling for the blessed gods. And she brought forth Hills, graceful haunts of the Nymphs who dwell amongst the glens."

SPARTA:
THE SOCIALIST EXPERIMENT

THE SPARTAN WAY

SPARTANS FORGED A TOUGH warrior culture that later people found admirable or repulsive. Their experiment with socialism (some would call it totalitarianism) depended on slaves to do all the work of farming and manufacturing, allowing Spartan male citizens to be full-time soldiers. The Spartan definition of citizen was restrictive, and based not just on a man's birth, but also his civic contributions. Each Spartan man received an allotment of land, and his slaves, called helots, needed to produce enough that the Spartan could contribute his share of crops for the community. If a Spartan missed his quota, he was kicked out, and became a *perioikos,* which literally means "a dweller round about"—not a slave, not a Spartan, but a peripheral person. A perioikos could not become a Spartan, so the number of citizens shrank over time, from dropouts and from deaths in battle. Citizens could be added only as children were born to Spartans, which made Spartan women vital to the community.

Spartan boys trained as soldiers from the time they could walk, and at age 7 moved to barracks. They lived with their teachers, and each bunk had names like "the cubs" or "the foxes." They ate in common mess halls, as their fathers did. They could marry at 20, but until age 30, men did not live with their wives. Instead, they remained in barracks.

Except for a poet or two who wrote marching songs, Spartans didn't leave any written record, so what we know about them comes from Athenian and later Roman writers. They describe how tough it was to grow up in Sparta. Boys slept on mattresses made of thorns, so they would not mind discomfort when camping on military raids. They were underfed, so they would learn to steal food quickly and quietly, as soldiers would scrounge for supplies. Boys were beaten publicly if they were found stealing food, not because it was immoral to steal, but because they weren't good enough at it to avoid being caught.

BRONZE HELMET: Corinthian type. Dedicated in 474 B.C. at Olympia.

HOPLITE: Hoplite running with spear and shield on a clay plaque. The word *kalos* ("Beauty") is written above.

INFANTICIDE

SPARTAN GIRLS WERE bred for reproduction. Women exercised in groups for as many hours a day as the men did, and were extra well fed, so they would give birth to strong future soldiers. Fitness training was mandatory and paid for by the state, in the name of prenatal care. Given the communal nature of their society, and that they shared food and shelter, maybe it is no surprise that Spartan citizens submitted their newborn boys to an examination before the council of elders. Allegedly, these elders looked for deformity, weakness, or low birth weight. (We know now that birth weight has little bearing on how strong or tall a boy would have grown up to be.) If the council determined that the infant was unfit for Spartan life, he would be thrown over a cliff. Spartan social expectations demanded that the mothers were not supposed to be sentimental about it.

Murdering a baby is called infanticide. As repulsive as it seems, the Spartans were not the only Greeks to kill their children. When the legendary Oedipus was born, an oracle predicted that he would usurp his father's throne. So his parents, Laius and Jocasta, left their baby out in a forest to die alone. A poor traveler found him and took him home to Corinth—so that he could indeed grow up and fulfill the oracle's prediction.

SPARTA: Archaeological site in foreground; modern city and Mount Taygetus in distance

THE HOPLITE REVOLUTION

THE SPARTANS ALL FOUGHT as equals, sharing the responsibility and the glory. They developed hoplite warfare, adopted quickly by most Greek city-states. Throughout the Mediterranean, Greek men fought the same way, in a kind of dance with rules, etiquette, and chivalry. A good Greek soldier stood his ground, protected his neighbor, and faced death with courage.

The phalanx was the block of soldiers standing close to each other, moving as one. The highest honor came from standing in the front line of the phalanx, protecting all the men behind. This interdependence in battle promoted friendship and loyalty among the group. The Greek shield, three feet in diameter, was called a *hoplon,* hence hoplites are the "Greeks holding shields." When the hoplites stood side by side in a phalanx, it looked like a metal wall on legs.

As the other city-states expanded their armies, some admitting every landowner as a hoplite, political rights needed to be extended to give

CHIGI VASE: Rows of hoplites fight in phalanx formation; a flute player gives the signal. From an Etruscan grave, 640 B.C.

SPARTAN MOTHERS AND SONS

"COME BACK WITH YOUR SHIELD—or on it," is the best known admonition from Plutarch's collection, "Sayings of Spartan Women." The Spartan warrior code of honor required that soldiers never turn their backs on the enemy or get struck from behind, as that would mean they were running away. Dropping a shield—coming back without it—also would mean that a man had fled the battlefield.

And how about "on it"? Hoplites used shields as stretchers to take the wounded and dead off the battlefield. What would happen to a boy who "lost" his shield but made it back to Sparta? Mom took care of that. "Because Damatria heard that her son was a coward and not worthy of her, she killed him when he arrived," according to Plutarch.

Another mother said, upon learning of her son's cowardice, "Worthless runt that you are, vile remnant, be off now to Hades: Off! For there is no way I bore this son, so unworthy of Sparta!"

them a share of power. This is known as the hoplite revolution: In the eighth century B.C., the adoption of hoplite warfare led to a political structure that, in most city-states, was more democratic. Larger armies of all landowners, fighting in phalanx formation, meant a mixing of income brackets in camaraderie.

When two hoplite armies faced each other, each first tried to intimidate the enemy so that they would retreat and no one would die that day. This could be done by singing loudly, yelling, beating shields, and even running toward the enemy. This intimidation made one side retreat more often than not. Think of it like a football game, where the quarterback calls time-out after seeing how the opponent's offense has lined up.

HELMETED DEATH MASK: From a mid-sixth century B.C. warrior's grave near Pella, Macedonia

If intimidation didn't work, the battle was on. A trumpet sounded, and the front ranks tried to stab each other with their spears, holding them high and aiming for necks or other vulnerable spots. The first stage of battle was called "the pushing." The back of the phalanx pressed on the men ahead of them, giving momentum all the way up to the front line. The goal was to punch through the middle. Breaking through would frighten the enemy and speed their defeat.

Most battles lasted less than an hour, which was about as much as anyone could take in the hot Greek sun. Short or long, though, hoplite battles left everyone a bloody mess. Dust, sweat, blood, noise, fear, and adrenaline exhausted the soldiers. ❖

CHAPTER III

BRIGHT, SHINING MOMENT

508 B.C.

Athens invents democracy

490 B.C.

Persian invasion stopped by
Battle of Marathon

480–479 B.C.

Greeks win Persian War

479–432 B.C.

Peak of Athenian power

432–421 B.C.

Peloponnesian War

415–413 B.C.

Sicilian expedition fails

413–404 B.C.

Sparta wins
Peloponnesian War

371 B.C.

Thebes defeats Sparta

359 B.C.

Philip II of Macedon
becomes king

338 B.C.

Macedonians defeat Greece at
the Battle of Chaeronea

336 B.C.

Alexander the Great

323 B.C.

The Hellenistic period begins

THE CLASSICAL PERIOD
508–323 B.C.

THE ATHENIANS ADOPTED A NEW CONSTITUTION in 508 B.C. that brought democratic representation and transparency into being. The Persian War, though, almost doomed their fledgling system. The Greeks held strong, even though the Persians devastated much of Greece before it was all over. Although small wars preoccupied some of the city-states afterward, the arts and literature blossomed, philosophy advanced, and scientific innovations and inventions proliferated. They built a culture of reflection, contemplation, civil discourse, and critical thinking, as well as reverence for freedom, justice, and the rule of law.

We call this the classical period, when Greek art reached its apex in the fifth and fourth centuries B.C. The Greeks perfected their style of architecture then, as seen in buildings like the Parthenon in Athens. In this period, bronze and marble statues represented gods like humans, and humans like gods.

This chapter focuses on the Greek achievements and the foundation of their success during this age. The Peloponnesian War, as Greeks fought Greeks from 432 to 404 B.C., slowed but did not stop their humanistic pursuits and other achievements that have long survived. What was it about these people and the way they lived that made them so creative, inventive, and open to new ideas?

ENTRANCE TO THE ACROPOLIS: *(opposite)* The dark stone course below the three steps marks the boundary of the sacred rock. WINE CUP: *(right)* A king supervises a factory on an interior of a *kylix* from Cyrene, Libya.

THE IONIAN REVOLT

THE PERSIAN WARS in many ways made the Greeks into "the Greeks." For the previous 50 years, the vast Persian Empire had been expanding west from its heartland in Iran; by 500 B.C. it extended from Afghanistan to Turkey. It had absorbed, through acquiescence or combat, the Levant, Egypt, and the Greek colonies in Ionia, on the west coast of Turkey, also known as Asia Minor. The Persians had even crossed the Dardanelles to take the region of Thrace and had made a pact with Macedonian kings.

Initially it seems the Persians did not intend to expand farther west to take over mainland Greece, but the Ionians revolted, changing that. Inspired by the new democratic ideas of people power and equality under the law, a few leaders of the Ionian Greek cities asked the other Greek cities to help them overthrow their Persian overlords. Mainland Greek interference between 499 and 493 B.C. brought Athenians in particular to the attention of King Darius I (the Great), because they sent 20 ships to aid the rebellion. His attendant would repeat after each meal, "Sire, remember the Athenians."

The Greeks helped the Ionian city-states try to rise up against the Persians because of their own determination to remain free, civilized, and self-governed. Throughout time they had battled to retain their own values, defining themselves by contrast with "the other," as West had fought East in the Trojan War. Even in their myths, the Greeks fought the centaurs, battled the Amazons, and outwitted the Cyclops. The Greeks framed the fight against the Persians in these same symbolic terms, casting themselves as the defenders of civilization against the barbarians in the rest of the ancient world.

In 492 B.C., a Persian army crossed the Dardanelles to try to attack Greece in retribution for the failed attempt to liberate Asia Minor. The army was primarily made up of conscripts, slaves, and mercenaries, rather than free men defending their homeland; this would ultimately

PERSIAN RIDER, ACROPOLIS: Rider wears Persian leggings in fragmentary marble statue.

DARIUS I: Marble portrait from royal palace at Persepolis, Iran

PERSIAN ARCHER: Helmet shape and leggings identify this warrior as Persian.

HOPLITE FIGHTS PERSIAN: Hand-to-hand combat between hoplite and Persian on interior of a kylix

make a tremendous difference. Weather turned them back, but the warning sign was clear—the Persians were bent on revenge for the aid the Greeks gave the Ionians in their uprising. King Darius said, "I'll be back."

At that time, in 492 B.C., there was no one single "Greek army." Had the weather not intervened, Greece would have been caught unprepared, and probably would have been defeated. If the Greeks lost, they would have been assimilated into the Persian Empire.

All Greek cities had their own armies, based on the hoplite phalanx. Some trained more than others, with Sparta having the only professional army. Few had navies, except for some Greek islands and the towns in Sicily. Rarely had two city-states collaborated in battle. Getting all the Greeks together to face an outside threat looked impossible, at least at the beginning. In 490 B.C., a larger Persian force crossed over into Greece, posing the greatest threat to the Greek people so far.

THE BATTLE OF MARATHON

IN CONTRAST TO THE PERSIANS, there was no king, no single general, really no one man with authority to declare war on behalf of the Greeks. Each city-state had to decide what it was going to do: join a coalition, stay back and prepare a defense, or ignore the fighting and pray for the best.

The Greeks did not believe that the full might of Persia would come down on them, and thus they were unprepared for the Persian invasion. It shocked them that the Persians actually were landing in mainland Greece, near Athens. The Athenian general Miltiades sent his best runner, Pheidippides, to ask Sparta for reinforcements. They could have really used the help from the most professional army in Greece. Pheidippides ran 150 miles in a day. The Spartan kings sent him back with the message that they would come after their religious festival ended. Conveniently, they arrived a day too late, after the battle ended.

The coalition of the willing gathered to face the Persians at Marathon, on the coast of Attica about 26 miles from Athens. However, they mustered only 10,000 troops, most of whom were Athenians or Plataeans, because other city-states did not perceive the invasion as a direct threat. They couldn't have been more wrong.

The Persians had 25,000 men and 600 ships. Their numbers made them terrifying foes. So did their strange clothing. Whereas the Greek soldiers wore a tunic with a pleated skirt, and a metal breastplate, a helmet, shield, and spear, plus greaves to protect the lower legs, the Persians wore woven pajamas and leather caps, and carried bows and arrows. To a Greek hoplite, they looked formidable and frightening. Who had ever seen men wearing pants?

The Persian ships docked, and warriors disembarked to

BATTLE OF MARATHON: Persians are the blue team on the right, Greeks in red on the left (1889).

assemble along the marshy coast. The Athenians, outnumbered more than two to one, charged at the Persians, unexpectedly. According to the historian, Herodotus, "The Persians, seeing them come at a run, made ready to receive them; but they believed that the Athenians were possessed by some very desperate madness, seeing their small numbers and their running to meet their enemies without the support of cavalry or archers. That was what the barbarians thought, but the Athenians, when they came hand-to-hand fighting, fought right worthily."

It was a long battle, but the Greeks pulled it off and cut the Persians down as they fled to their ships; 6,400 Persians died. Afraid that the Persian ships would sail to Athens, Miltiades again dispatched Pheidippides to run the 26 miles from the battlefield to Athens, to tell the civic leaders of the victory. When the runner arrived, he uttered "Joy, we won!" Then he collapsed, dying on the spot.

ATHENIANS DEBATE WAR

IN ATHENS, ONLY THE ASSEMBLY of all landowning male citizens had the power to approve civic funds to go to war. Speaking before the Athenian assembly, the minister of war, Callimachus, led a fairly strong coalition of aristocrats who did not believe it was necessary to fight. Miltiades, who became the general of the Greeks at Marathon, persuaded his opponent and his supporters with these words, according to Herodotus: "It now depends on you, Callimachus, either to enslave Athens, or, by preserving its liberty, to leave a memorial of yourself to every age . . . The opinions

HELMET OF MILTIADES, OLYMPIA

of us generals, who are ten, are equally divided; the one party urging that we should engage, the other that we should not. All these things now entirely depend on you. For if you will support my opinion, your country will be free, and the city the first city in Greece; but if you join with those who would dissuade us from the engagement, the contrary of the advantages I have enumerated will fall to your lot."

Miltiades's speech was persuasive. Callimachus supported the vote to go to war, and the assembly voted to appropriate funds and levy troops. Alongside Miltiades, Callimachus served as a general. He was one of the 192 Greeks who died in battle, but the Athenians and their allies were victorious.

ON SHIPS AND SILVER

IN THE TEN YEARS BETWEEN the victory at Marathon in 490 B.C. and the second round of the Persian Wars, the Greeks needed to figure out what to do. Might the Persians return? Considering that the Greeks would likely be outnumbered again, and that their liberty might depend on fighting at sea as well as on land, the idea of building ships might seem obvious. But it took an extraordinary statesman to make the proposal and to win the people's support.

That man was Themistocles, a politician who was not born into the aristocracy. Just a few years after the victory at Marathon, a vein of silver was discovered south of Athens. As a democracy, the people got to decide what to do with the silver. Someone proposed a handout of ten drachmas to every Athenian. People liked this idea. But Themistocles made a different proposal: Athens should prepare to defend itself. He gave the speech of his life, persuading the Athenians to invest the funds to build 200 of the great battle ships called triremes. This speech, this vote saved Greece from having to surrender to Persian rule ten years later—and so saved Western civilization.

At the beginning of the fifth century B.C., there was yet no invention of the genres of history or drama, no Parthenon, no flowering of creativity in the future university town of Athens. Had the Persians prevailed, Greek culture would have been stunted. The Greeks as we think of them would have assimilated into the culture of the Persian Empire. This speech, this vote made all the difference.

Triremes were the backbone of the Greek navy, with 170 rowers manning each one. Each ship had three decks of oarsmen, crews that stroke in sync with the sounds of pipes and calls. Free men worked the oars. They camped, slept, ate, and rowed together day after day, training and patrolling, honing their skills as they prepared for battle. Camaraderie developed among the rowers, who were of the lower class. Many craftsmen and small traders supplied the ships and crew, also benefiting from the new military economy. Back in Iran, King Darius I had died and his son Xerxes took the throne. When the new great king of Persia decided it was time for round two in 480 B.C., this time, the Greeks were prepared.

OSTRACON OF THEMISTOCLES: Athenians wrote names on ostraca (broken potsherds) to nominate leaders for ostracism.

SHIP AT SEA: (opposite) Dolphins chase Dionysus on his ship, its mast entwined with vines.

THERMOPYLAE AND CAPE ARTEMISION

Tᴀᴇ sᴘᴀʀᴛᴀɴs ʟᴇꜰᴛ ꜰᴇᴡ ʀᴇᴄᴏʀᴅs, and those were about war, like this exhortation from the Spartan poet Tyrtaeus:

Go forth, children of citizens of Sparta,
the land of brave men.
With left hand
the shield put forward firmly,
The spear raised with your right
Go forth and show your courage
without fearing for your life
Because fear for one's own life
does not become a Spartan.

When the Persians returned in 480 B.C., the Greeks decided to hold them by sea at the northern tip of the island of Euboea, called Cape Artemision, and on land at the pass of Thermopylae. Themistocles commanded the fleet, and the Spartan army under Leonidas took the pass. The pass was so narrow that the vast Persian numbers had little advantage. It reduced the battle to hand-to-hand combat, with Sparta, the most professional army in Greece, defending their country against a massive Persian army made up of conscripts, mercenaries, and slaves.

For two solid days, 3,000 Greeks led by Leonidas and his 300 men cut down the Persians, whose numbers might have been 200,000 or more. Then a traitor showed the Persians a secret goat trail around that pass, and the army ran through down into the plain below. When it was clear all was lost, Leonidas told the rest of the Greeks to go south to take up a new defensive position. He and his 300 Spartans would stay to cut down as many more Persians as they could. It is one of the most famous last stands in all history. The Spartans who defended the pass of Thermopylae are still remembered for their ultimate sacrifice. The epitaph on their tomb there reads "Go passersby, tell the Spartans we died here, obedient to her laws."

Themistocles heard about the loss while aboard his ship at Cape Artemision. The strategy had required both positions to hold. With the Persian army overrunning central Greece, Themistocles moved the navy to a new, more southerly position at Salamis. The Athenians had asked the Delphic oracle for a prophecy that would help them decide what to do between the two Persian invasions. The last two lines of the response had the ambiguous phrase "Divine Salamis, to women's sons you will bring death, when the wheat is scattered, or the harvest gathered." Themistocles convinced the Athenians that the death referenced was meant for the Persian sons, and Salamis would be their divine savior.

There were no other strategic places to stop the Persians until they reached the Peloponnese. Athens lay in between, exposed and indefensible. The Athenians evacuated to the Peloponnese, just before Persians sacked the city, burning and destroying. They smashed the Archaic marbles, now in the Acropolis Museum. Only later did the Athenians ceremonially bury these broken pieces on the Acropolis, to dispose of them without committing sacrilege. This sack of Athens was the pretext that Alexander the Great used for his own campaign against Persia 146 years later.

LEONIDAS, SPARTA: This marble bust, early fifth century B.C., was found near the Temple of Athena in Sparta.

BATTLE OF THERMOPYLAE: *(opposite)* In the foreground, combatants fight with spears, daggers, and arrows; the Persian line extends for miles.

THERMOPYLAE

THE PASS AT THERMOPYLAE was only 45 feet wide in the summer of 480 B.C. Visitors today may be puzzled. The pass is far wider now, with a highway running through. Geologists explain that the site sits on the crumbling edge of the Earth's crust, and that deposits of soil left by meandering rivers have moved the coastline some three to five miles out over the 2,500 years that have passed.

Herodotus said that the Greek side had 7,100 troops, and the Persian side had 2.5 million, plus that many camp followers. This number seems unbelievable, which is why later historians tend to lower the estimate. Even a fourth of that number pouring over the pass at Thermopylae with only 300 Spartans left to stop them is barely imaginable. Like the Allies at Gallipoli in World War I, the Spartans knew they wouldn't make it, but still gave their all. Leonidas and his 300 were instant heroes, and their sacrifice is remembered to this day.

SALAMIS AND THE END OF THE PERSIAN WAR

ONCE THERMOPYLAE WAS LOST, the geography offered no other place to block the Persians except the two-mile-wide isthmus between the mainland and the Peloponnese. It was inevitable that Athens would be sacked. The Athenians voted to evacuate, leaving behind some old men and people unwilling to leave who moved up to the Acropolis. The rest settled in the Peloponnese at a place called Troizene while the warriors went with Themistocles to Salamis. When the Persians came, those who stayed behind on the Acropolis were burned alive.

Ship for ship, the Greek navy was still no match for the Persian fleet, but Themistocles had a plan. The Greek navy could lure the Persian fleet into the narrow straits of Salamis off the coast of Attica, where Greece's triremes would sink the ships one by one. After a long debate, the Athenians voted in favor of the plan, then made it work.

PERSIAN BODYGUARDS: Heavily armed archers on a glazed brick wall of the king's palace at Susa, Iran

They positioned the Greek triremes between the island of Salamis and the coast in a narrow, C-shaped waterway. To win, the Persians would have to attack the Greek ships in this narrow passage, just as their soldiers had done at Thermopylae. The Persian great king Xerxes pitched a tent on a high hill overlooking the bay, as his servants presented rich food on gold and silver plates. He had seats in the skybox for what he thought would be an amusing victory. This time, though, there was no traitor to show the Persians how to get around the Greek lines. Instead, in a fierce fight, the Greek naval forces triumphed.

One final battle remained. At Plataea in 479 B.C., the Greeks defeated the Persians again. The armies of 31 allies met the Persian army under the leadership of Pausanias of Sparta. The Greek city of Thebes sided with the Persians, angering the rest of the Greeks. The Greek side had the largest army it had ever assembled, perhaps as many as 60,000 men. Again the Greeks attacked at a run, routing their opponents. The Persian Wars were over. The Theban commanders were executed without trial. As the Greeks stripped the Persian soldiers of their armor and took possession of the king's tents, they found wealth beyond measure.

ODYSSEUS AND THE CYCLOPS

CYCLOPS BLINDED

WE CAN STILL SEE most elements of Greek character and culture in the epics of Homer. The story of the Cyclops embodies the clash of civilized heroes versus barbaric foes. Odysseus and his men, stranded on the island where the barbaric Cyclops lived as a shepherd, became trapped in his cave. The Cyclops began to eat the men one by one as snacks. Odysseus had to figure out what to do. After getting the Cyclops drunk on wine, he sharpened a stick and poked the giant's eye out. The survivors tied themselves to the underbellies of his sheep, so that when the now blind giant counted the sheep by patting them, the men could escape unnoticed.

To an ancient Greek, the lesson of this tale was that even when the odds are against you, when the enemy is larger than you, there is always a way to win if you use ingenuity and imagination. After all, this is how they won at Marathon and Salamis and bought themselves time at Thermopylae.

Many craftsmen painted this scene on vases. The public bought the ceramics for their homes, so they could pass the tale of Odysseus and the Cyclops on through the generations, because this story can be read on so many levels, appreciated by children and statesmen alike.

A war memorial for the battle of Plataea survives in Istanbul. A golden tripod (now missing), with a base made of three bronze snakes that have survived, was dedicated to Apollo at Delphi, with the names of the 31 Greek city-states inscribed on it. In the fourth century A.D., Constantine the Great brought the monument from Delphi to what was then Constantinople, where it can still be seen in the hippodrome. The inscription once engraved on the golden tripod, now missing, read, "This is the gift the saviors of far-flung Greece upraised here [at Delphi] having delivered their states from loathsome slavery's bonds." That was memorized and repeated through the centuries to memorialize this triumph. Without this victory, Persia might have absorbed Greece into its empire, and with that, the creativity and artistic expression that we associate with the height of Greek civilization would have been lost.

WARSHIP: Greek relief of an Athenian trireme from the Acropolis in Athens

SHAKING UP SOCIETY: BIRTH OF THE ATHENIAN DEMOCRACY

I N 508 B.C., the citizens of Athens were mired in legislative gridlock and bitter animosity. There was unrest in the streets, and the city was so weak and dysfunctional it had become intolerable, even to the elites. The Council of 400 and the Assembly asked Cleisthenes, a well-connected man who was what we would call a political consultant, to fix the problem. Looking closely, he saw that several leading families in different areas of Attica controlled blocs of voters who lived near them. Maybe one family owed them money. Maybe another needed to borrow some oxen. Maybe still others had worked for them. These people were now expected to vote as the aristocrat dictated. Each generation remained obligated. This had to stop.

Cleisthenes got to work. He rearranged the political organization of Athens from its traditional four ancestral tribes to ten. He wanted to make sure that the aristocratic families could no longer control their regions when it came time to vote in the assemblies. To do this, he first took a population survey of the peninsula of Attica. Next, he reassigned every citizen to one of the ten brand-new tribes. Each tribe was a mixture of an equal number of people who lived on the coast, the hills, and the plain. These tribes enrolled recent immigrants as well. Many people had moved from other city-states to Athens in the sixth and early fifth centuries B.C., and not being from old families, they had been left out of the tribes.

Mixing people from different areas meant that there was more diversity inside each tribe. The coast people were interested in policies that affected trade or fishing. Hill people were concerned with manufacturing and crafts. The people of the plain were mainly farmers. Now they all had to talk to each other, compromise, and negotiate. It released the tribes from the grip of any one aristocratic family. It gave the *demos*

CLEISTHENES: Modern bust depicts the Athenian credited with founding democracy; Ohio Statehouse, 2004.

("people") its *kratia* ("power"), from which our word today is derived—"democracy."

In ancient city-states, individuals belonged to many different social groups, and the mixing meant exposure to people with new and different ideas. In addition to Cleisthenes's mixed tribes, men joined informal brotherhoods that cut across the geographical boundaries. Clusters of people were also united by trades, religious cults, military units, schools, and more, weaving the complex fabric of Athenian society. Such open but interconnected systems tended to support and encourage tolerance and creativity, and allow new ideas to flourish.

Cleisthenes also changed the membership in the Council from 400 elected members (100 men from each of the four ancestral tribes) to 500 men selected by lottery (50 men from each of the ten tribes). The Council of 500 met in the Athenian agora in a newly built council house. All month they would receive people's complaints or proposals, and at the end of the month they decided which issues to put before the people's Assembly for debate and perhaps a vote. The Council of 500 only had the authority to set the agenda for the people's Assembly, who made all the final decisions. As the Assembly was not a representative body but consisted of all male freeborn citizens, this again puts the power in the people's hands. This was the birth of democracy in Athens.

PERICLES: The political leader and general who succeeded Cleisthenes, Themistocles, and Cimon in guiding Athens

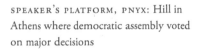

SPEAKER'S PLATFORM, PNYX: Hill in Athens where democratic assembly voted on major decisions

A NEW DEAL FOR ATHENS

THE CRITERION FOR RUNNING for elected office in mid-fifth-century Athens was merit. Opportunities were available to almost anybody who could qualify and serve well—women, slaves, and the landless poor excluded.

Pericles, who appeared on the scene in the 460s, said that poverty was nothing to be ashamed of; the important thing was to do something about it. Yet poverty continued to pull many people away from participating in democratic assemblies or standing for the lottery to serve on a jury, because they needed to work or because they lived too far from the city. Pericles came from an old and wealthy family but chose a career in public service and was an advocate for the working poor. He introduced legislation that provided a daily wage to anyone who served as a juror. As more people from a variety of backgrounds participated in civic life, it diluted the influence of the aristocrats.

Such experiments made Athens an inspiration to people in other towns, some of which were governed by tyrants or oligarchies. Internal struggles for power erupted all over Greece, with democrats lobbying for expanded rights, and asking Athens for support. As this kept

PARTHENON: View of Acropolis from its entrance, the Propylaea, as it looked in 1871

THE FOUR ECONOMIC CLASSES

FAMILIES WERE RANKED in four economic classes. From the early sixth century B.C. members of the top two classes were eligible for public posts. The wealthiest were called the 500 bushel holders, meaning they owned enough land to cultivate 500 bushels of crops a year, an indication of the agrarian roots of wealth. The second class, the *equites* or "knights," were wealthy enough to own horses. Craftsmen, traders, and small farmers formed the third class, and the landless poor were at the bottom. Most people fell into the third and fourth classes, and the upper two usually voted together as aristocrats. But some wealthy men such as Solon, Cleisthenes, Cimon, and Pericles advocated for the masses, and under Pericles the Assembly passed new laws that allowed even the third class to run for the highest offices.

happening, the aristocrats would call on Sparta for help. Eventually, this cycle of proxy fighting from the 450s to 432 B.C. escalated into the Peloponnesian War.

Meanwhile, tribute money kept flowing into Athens from the other city-states. Aristotle, writing a century later, explained how many people were put to work because of those funds: "For the combined proceeds of the tributes and the taxes and the allies served to feed more than 20,000 men. For there were 6,000 jurymen, 1,600 archers and also 1,200 cavalry, 500 members of the Council, 500 guardians of the docks, and also 50 watchmen in the city, as many as 700 officials at home and as many as 700 abroad; and in addition to these, when later they settled into the war, 2,500 hoplites, 20 guard-ships and other ships conveying the guards to the number of 200 elected by lot; and furthermore . . . orphans, and warders of prisoners—for all of these had their maintenance from public funds."

ATHENIAN OWL: Tribute from allies was paid with coins such as this silver Athenian tetradrachm, showing the owl of Athens; sixth century B.C.

Pericles also proposed a public building program, a kind of stimulus package that resulted in the construction of the Parthenon, so that men without skills could learn a trade by working as rope makers, wagon builders, quarrymen, or sculptors. After the projects were completed in 432 B.C., each of those men who had been without skills and unemployed in 450 B.C. now had the opportunity to earn a good salary and teach his trade to his sons.

TERM LIMITS AND TRANSPARENCY STARTED HERE

T HE ATHENIANS WANTED TO avoid tyranny or one-man rule at all costs, and thus they invented or adopted the ideas of rotation, accountability, and the use of the lottery. Rotation means term limits. No one could hold the same office for more than a year, except for the members of the Areopagus court (their version of the Supreme Court), who held their posts for life. Everyone else rotated out. People could serve twice in a lifetime.

Another safeguard against tyranny was for committees to make all decisions rather than letting one man, unsupervised, gain too much prestige. All city jobs, paid or not, from army general to sewer commissioner, were staffed by ten men, one from each tribe. Ten people had to make every decision. It boosted accountability, but it's a wonder anything got done.

KLEROTERION: Identification cards were put in columns by tribe for selection by lottery.

These committees were selected by lottery, one man from each tribe for a board of ten. Only generals and treasurers were elected by public vote. Generals, when you think about it, needed skills and experience, so the lottery was not ideal for that. Pericles was one of ten elected generals, reelected 15 years straight, but one year he was voted out, then reelected the next year. Treasurers needed some math skills, so they were elected exclusively from the two wealthiest economic classes.

RHAMNOUS: One of 140 villages (demes) in Attica, united in the polis of Athens

Use of the lottery to select people to serve in civic offices and on juries became standard practice in Athens. To conduct the lotteries, the Athenians used a clever machine called a *kleroterion,* an upright marble slab with ten columns of slots. On selection day, anyone who wanted to serve in an office would put his identification card in a slot under the name of his tribe, thus creating horizontal rows of cards, one from each tribe. When the grid was full, white and black balls were fed into a cone. The balls randomly dropped down into a tube next to the slots. As each ball dropped, a row of people's identification cards would be rejected or accepted, depending on whether the ball that came out of the tube was black (rejected) or white (accepted). If a row was selected, all ten men would be that year's board of supervisors, or sanitary commission, or archons (like mayors), or whatever officers were being chosen at that time. Think of how radical this is—the Athenians trusted each other enough to let the machine select their magistrates.

These machines were also used to select jurors, in which case they didn't select just ten men, but 50 to 1,500, depending on the case. Selection by lottery was interpreted as being chosen by the gods, whose will it was to select or reject each row. Losers accepted the result with grace, knowing it was divine will.

NOMINATIONS
ON OSTRACA

FEELING LEFT OUT? TRY OSTRACISM

PERIODICALLY, THE ATHENIAN people expelled powerful individuals who seemed to pose a threat to democracy. They sent them away for ten years, but their families could stay behind and they didn't lose their property. When the exiles returned, they were out of the loop. Their social networks were weaker and older, and most of the pressing political issues from their day had long been resolved.

How did it work? Over the course of a specific three-week period, Athenians would consider who, if anyone, ought to be ostracized. On decision day, citizens brought to the city center broken potsherds (the Greek word is ostracon). At home or on the way, they scratched a name onto the piece of clay. When they got downtown, they would drop the piece into a box. If any one person's name appeared on 6,000 or more potsherds, he would be ostracized. Many excavated ostraca have the names of the most famous people of Athenian history, although not all were actually ostracized because some fell short of the required 6,000 votes.

THE ATHENIAN EMPIRE

AFTER DEFEATING THE PERSIANS in 479 B.C., the Greeks met to decide how to protect themselves. The Spartan kings boycotted the emergency session, anxious about committing to long months of patrolling on sea instead of land where they were most comfortable, and perhaps worried their men could hear too much about those newfangled inventions called democracy and free speech. The people living in coastal towns and islands were most at risk if the Persians returned, so they joined a defensive pact to keep the Persians away by patrolling the Aegean Sea. We call it the Delian League, because the annual dues each member city-state contributed were kept on the island of Delos, conveniently located in the middle of the Cyclades. The tribute payments covered the costs of patrol boats and sailors, plus a 10 percent administration fee to Apollo's sanctuary at Delos.

Each city-state could choose how to pay its dues, either in cash or by sending ships or sailors. Over time, the allies opted to send money and keep their boys home. The tribute paid for 20,000 Athenians to work on the ships or to support the seafaring with provisions and materials such as rope, sailcloth, storage baskets, food, and armor.

Within about 20 years, Athens alone was providing the ships and men, and the Athenian Empire was born. Dues went to Delos, the funds were brought to Athens, and the wages were paid to Athenian sailors and suppliers. Once the Athenian economy became so dependent on Delian League funds, the now well-armed Athenians had to ensure that the tribute kept coming. They besieged city-states that tried to stop paying.

A turning point came when Pericles led a Delian League expedition south to Egypt, where the Egyptians were revolting against their Persian overlords. Athenians liked to promote democracy abroad by supporting rebellions in places under tyrannical regimes. From 459 to 454 B.C., as the Egyptians suffered losses, so did the Athenians, and when the Persians regained control, Athens went home. The Delian League members, afraid that the Persians would retaliate and capture Delos, voted to move their treasury to Athens. Now Athena's priests got the 10 percent administrative fee, plus kept all the cash on the Acropolis. That gave Athens complete control of the Delian League.

ATHENS: The Parthenon, viewed from the Propylaea, protected the Delian League treasury.

WAR: *(opposite)* Naval warfare was confusing, frightening, and expensive. Delian League tribute paid the costs.

HOW THE DELIAN LEAGUE
BECAME THE ATHENIAN EMPIRE

THE ISLANDS AND COASTAL CITY-STATES joined the Delian League willingly in 478 B.C. because they were genuinely scared the Persians might return a third time. At first, the Delian League met as a representative council for mutual protection. Only when Athens ended up doing all the work, and controlling all the money, did the Delian League become the heavy-handed Athenian Empire. As Thucydides wrote,

> Of all the causes of defection [from the Delian League], that connected with arrears of tribute and vessels, and with failure of service, was the chief; for the Athenians were very severe and exacting, and made themselves offensive by applying the screw of necessity to men who were not used to and in fact not disposed for any continuous labor. In some other respects the Athenians were not the old popular rulers they had been at first; and if they had more than their fair share of service, it was correspondingly easy for them to reduce any that tried to leave the confederacy. For this the allies had themselves to blame, their wish to get out of giving service making most leave their homes. Thus while Athens was increasing her navy with the funds which they contributed, a revolt always found them without resources or experience for war.

INTERNATIONAL TRAVEL AND TRADE IN THE MEDITERRANEAN WORLD

WINE CUP: A woman pours wine for seated elder. Wine was a major commodity for trade in the Mediterranean.

THE ANCIENT GREEKS TRAVELED for many reasons. Religious festivals drew pilgrims and athletes to sanctuaries such as Delphi or Olympia. Oracles beckoned civic leaders to the remote site of Dodona in northwestern Greece or to the Siwa Oasis in Egypt. People traveled to study with famous philosophers at Miletus and Pergamon. Physicians trained on the island of Kos. Southern Italy and Sicily were called Magna Graecia—greater Greece—because there was so much interaction and shared history. Ambassadors and messengers moved among the cities constantly. All this back-and-forth tied people together in the Greek world in social ways.

Many people moved to Athens, drawn to expanded opportunities and to its port. By 431 B.C., about 22,000 Athenian male citizens owned land; at the same time, there were about 28,000 resident aliens. In other words, there were more foreigners than male landowners.

Greeks sailed the seas and traded with international partners, who themselves sailed into mainland Greek ports with their goods. Greek innovations stemmed from visiting cities abroad, and Greeks had an open mind for learning from foreigners, bringing back new ideas in addition to imported goods.

Foreigners and returning merchants imported perfumes, glass, barley, wheat, rugs, bronze, silver, gold, and ivory. They traded with places including Sicily, Arabia, Egypt, and Ethiopia. Greek pottery has been found in Israel.

Greece's main exports were olive oil, wine, pottery, and metalwork. Many Etruscan tombs north of Rome contained ceramic vases manufactured in Greece, mainly Athens and Corinth. Fabrics of women who worked the looms were traded as well.

The Greeks and their Mediterranean trade network behaved like a living complex adaptive system, in which the interdependent members responded and learned from outside events, and with resilience, grew and thrived. This trade network lasted for about 1,000 years. Unlike the situation back in the Bronze Age, it never really collapsed, but waxed and waned, even through Roman times, slowing down and not ending until the Roman Empire divided into East and West around the fourth century A.D.

EARRINGS
Granulated gold hoop earrings with
Pegasus on a crescent; from Volos,
Greece, fourth or third century B.C.

GOLD HAIRNET
Gold-and-enamel medallion features a
relief bust of Artemis; third century B.C.

GOLD MEDALLION
Gorgon's head with wings. Volos,
third to second century B.C.

AMPHORA
Three men weigh merchandise
for sale using industrial scales;
mid-sixth century B.C.

OIL FLASK
Women weaving woolen fabric
or carpet on a warp-weighted loom;
540 B.C.

JEWELRY BOX
A seated woman spins yarn; another
holds a small hand loom; 430 B.C.

LEST WE FORGET

HISTORY IS ABOUT MEMORY. As Herodotus, the first true historian, wrote at the start of his prose account of the Persian Wars, "This publication of the research of Herodotus of Halicarnassus is presented so that the memory of what men have done is hereby preserved from decay, and to prevent the great and wonderful actions of the Greeks and the barbarians from losing their due share of glory; and that the causes may be remembered for which these waged war with one another."

Greek funerary markers, trophy monuments, inscriptions on stone, and gifts to the gods at sanctuaries all point to one thing: Greek people wanted to be remembered. As individuals and as city-states, they wanted to leave a lasting mark. Collective civic monuments were focal points. The tumulus or mound at Marathon contained the remains of the 192 Athenians who died in the fight there against the Persians. Back in Athens, stone stelae, or upright slabs on bases, were engraved with epigrams, along with casualty lists, and erected in the public graveyard. Several of these poems commemorating deaths in the Persian and Pelo- ponnesian Wars have survived. Reading them tells us how friends and families remembered these soldiers and sailors, and how later genera- tions would recall them.

After the Battle of Salamis, the Athenians gathered their dead as best they could from the Aegean Sea, and in the collective tumulus they left a stone inscription to commemorate the fallen. It said:

> *The excellence of these men will shine an imperishable*
> *light forever*
> *On those to whom the gods assign rewards for great deeds;*
> *For on foot and on swift sailing ships they prevented*
> *All Greece from seeing a day of slavery.*

Inscribed on marble, these dedications were designed to last forever. Notice the strong words "shine an imperishable light." Around the same time, the Corinthians also set up a monument for their war dead on Salamis. Their inscription reads, "When all Greece was balanced on the razor's edge, we protected her with our souls and here we lie."

At funerals, the speakers emphasized the courage and valor of the fallen. After the first year of the Peloponnesian War in 431 B.C., Pericles gave the speech commemorating all the Athenians who had died in battle that year. Thucydides included a version of the speech in his history of the war, and we now call it Pericles' Funeral Oration: "For the whole earth is the grave of famous men, and not only does the inscription on stones at home mark them, but the unwritten memory of their attitude rather than their deed dwells in each person's mind."

FALLEN WARRIOR, AEGINA: Architectural sculpture, Temple of Athena

HOW DID THE GREEKS TELL TIME?

THE ANCIENT GREEKS TOLD TIME from the position of the sun. Early on, sundials did the trick. In public areas such as courts and markets, people consulted a *klepsydra,* or water clock. A square stone pit was filled with water at a steady pace. A flag floated up top, and the sides of the tub were marked with the hours. Unlike a sundial, it worked in the dark.

It was more complicated to say what year it was. The first Olympiad meant (our) 776 B.C., the traditional date of the first games. The second Olympiad was four years later. To refer to an event in 548 B.C., one could say it happened in the 59th Olympiad. To refer to an event inside a particular city, the name of the chief magistrate at the time could be used. The list was available to the public, but wasn't exactly handy. That method worked only at a very local level, where people recalled who was in charge when.

THE FUTURE ORIENTATION
OF THE GREEKS

THE GREEKS KNEW WE were coming. They anticipated that future generations would want to know who they were and what they did. Their arts and letters are time capsules, deliberately created for our benefit. No earlier civilization wrote for future ages to the degree that the ancient Greeks did. In Pericles' Funeral Oration, one memorable line says, "Future ages will wonder at us, as the present age wonders at us now."

Thucydides speaks directly to us when he says, "For if the cities of Athens and Sparta were to be buried, and only the foundations remained of its buildings, people would think Sparta was half as powerful as she really was, and Athens twice as powerful." He is contrasting the Spartan lifestyle versus the Athenian one, but we see an eerie archaeological way of looking at his time from our perspective.

Thucydides recorded the history of the Peloponnesian War because he believed he was witnessing world-shaking events that future ages

ATHENIAN ACROPOLIS: View from southwest; behind is Lycabettus Hill, the highest point in Athens.

would need to understand. He thought that knowledge could prevent future conflict and that studying the war between the Spartan alliance and the Athenian Empire could prevent another war on such a scale, and thus felt a calling, a kind of responsibility, to capture, record, and preserve history for those students who weren't alive yet to witness it themselves. He wrote, "The absence of romance in my history will, I fear, detract somewhat from its interest; but if it be judged useful by those who desire an exact knowledge of the past as an aid to the interpretation of the future . . . I shall be content. In sum, I have written my work, not as an essay which is to win the applause of the moment, but as a possession for all time."

Grave markers can provide detailed insight into relationships and society, telling us how families wanted their loved ones to be remembered, and this included girls and women. In 1729, a French traveler copied down the inscription on an ancient statue base built into a chapel in the Athenian countryside: "The tomb of Phrasikleia. Maiden I will always be called, since instead of marriage this is what the gods have allotted. Aristion of Paros made it." Here she mourns her own future, that she would never marry. Here an unwed girl has an expectation that she will be remembered forever. Of course, in all actuality her parents or family paid for the monument and approved the text.

PHRASIKLEIA

PHRASIKLEIA THE ETERNAL MAIDEN

IN 1972, AN ARCHAEOLOGIST made an amazing find while excavating an ancient cemetery off a dead-end street in a village called Merenda, south of the new Athens airport. Almost perfectly preserved, Phrasikleia's marble feet fit perfectly into the hole on top of the inscribed statue base found in 1729. The lead "glue" that sealed the statue to the base was still around her feet. She is the best-preserved Greek statue of a woman, with the colors on her dress, jewelry, and hair still visible. Examination in 2008 with ultraviolet-visible absorption spectroscopy and x-ray fluorescence analysis showed 11 different colorants used, plus gold foil. The closed lotus bud in her hand symbolizes her virginity. Phrasikleia now is prominently displayed in the National Archaeological Museum in Athens. Her family wished for her to be remembered forever, and they would probably be thrilled to see her name and statue there.

KNOW THYSELF

THE ATHENIAN EDUCATION system became a model for the rest of Greece. The system developed in response to the needs of a participatory democracy, where adults had to understand policy proposals, speak publicly with persuasive elegance, and be able to do at least some basic math to understand war allocations and taxes.

The monthly Assembly, open to every male citizen of Athens, took place on an acoustically vibrant limestone outcropping northwest of the Acropolis, called the Pnyx. During the Assembly, any participant could stand before the crowd and speak for or against an idea. The Greeks called this *isegoria,* the right to speak in public, which became the basis for our freedom of speech.

To persuade the public to vote to go to war, to finance a temple, to pass legislation, to make a treaty, or to approve a budget, citizens had to make speeches. Not just average ones, but great ones that stirred people to action. Pericles was the original motivational speaker. In his most famous speech, known as the Funeral Oration, he said: "Anyone can discourse to you forever about the advantages of a brave defense, which you know already. But instead of listening to him I would have you day by day fix your eyes upon the greatness of Athens, until you become filled with the love of her; and when you are impressed by the spectacle of her glory, reflect that this empire has been acquired by men who knew their duty and had the courage to do it."

Over time, speech making, or the art of oratory, became necessary to rise in society. This meant that a lot of teachers of rhetoric found employment training Athenian youths. Teachers moved to Athens from all over the Greek world for jobs. The brain drain from cities in Asia Minor and Sicily was particularly significant. Thus, Athens became a university town as a result of the democratic reforms that required excellent public speaking abilities.

To understand audits and budgets, people needed to know how to count, add, subtract, and possibly divide and multiply. Geometry also originated because of the need to measure the earth for urban planning, zoning, and taxation (geo means "earth" and meter equals "measure"). Mathematics as a field developed in the fifth and fourth centuries B.C., with lasting impact. Pythagoras and Euclid, whose names are still linked to basic principles of geometry, are just two of the many Greek scientists who changed the world. When Cleisthenes did a census of all people in Attica in 508 B.C., in order to assign them to his ten new tribes, he needed support staff who could count in high numbers and who could write fluently.

The principle of accountability also helped Athenian democracy succeed. At the end of the year, anyone who had handled a budget was brought before the Council of 500 for an audit. This was much worse than being audited by the IRS, because you faced 500 people going through your books and grilling you, in public. The treasurers of Athena, an elected board of ten men, one from each tribe, were responsible for money and for the gold and silver urns, statues, and other offerings on the Acropolis, so they went through an especially detailed audit annually, called the scrutiny. The rest of the citizens wanted to make sure that every little thing was still there, that a tiny gold ring didn't accidentally slip into a pocket. The results of those audits were published on marble for all to see. These marble inscriptions list the items that were once in the Parthenon, which included gilt furniture, ritual knives, gold and silver vases and bowls, lyres, flutes, and jewelry, all of which have long since vanished. After the scrutiny, some treasurers were tried for embezzlement.

To become good citizens, children had to learn how to make good choices with ethical decision-making. They did so through conversations with mentors. Boys would take long walks with older youths or grown men, and using examples mainly from Homer's epics, they would discuss the ethics of a hero who could be a role model. Nestor, the wise adviser in *The Iliad,* was an example of good counsel and wisdom. Agamemnon was a strategist and leader who made very tough choices. Achilles, irrational and emotional, was also brilliant and brave. Odysseus used intelligence and cunning to accomplish his goals, but often lied or used tricks to get his way. Children (and adults) were immersed in this repertory of life lessons, in songs, poems, theatrical plays, and vase paintings.

AMPHORA: A youthful, well-dressed orator speaks, gesturing for dramatic effect.

AN ANCIENT GREEK EDUCATION

OST CITY-STATES HAD schools for boys up to age 14. The children memorized a lot, and corporal punishment for mistakes was common. Most girls did not receive formal schooling. They learned stories, songs, and skills like playing the flute or weaving at home. Many women could read, and some were poets and songwriters.

In the teen years, youths either went to work or, if they were wealthier, studied in courtyards surrounded by classrooms. In these palaestras, boys learned athletics, literature, and music to develop the body, mind, and soul in equal parts.

After school, the wealthiest boys had tutors for rhetoric to learn to be persuasive. The tutors were known as sophists, and some were famous. By the fifth century, a flood of sophists had moved to Athens. With so many teachers in town, boys could also take private lessons in philosophy, music, and mathematics. Families competed to get sons into the best schools—that is, hire the most famous tutors. The boys learned to use their advanced education to intimidate and manipulate people. As more elite boys became great speakers, fewer average citizens felt free to speak up in assemblies. Athens became less democratic.

PALAESTRA, OLYMPIA: *(opposite)*
Courtyard for lessons and athletic training

LOVE, GREEK STYLE

BUILT INTO THE UPBRINGING of upper-class Greeks was a tradition we would see as pederasty and child abuse, but that they thought of as normal. A father would match his own teen with a young adult, maybe eight to ten years older, to escort the boy around town, take him to the symposia (dinner parties), and be his role model. This big brother program usually

VASE DEPICTING MUSIC LESSON

included the boy's first sexual experiences, lasting until the boy became an adult. Then it was his turn to be the big brother. Once he reached 28 or so, he would then choose a wife (about 15 years of age) and marry her.

Sometimes sexual relations with men continued. Greek men of all ages openly talked about their crushes on youths. Vase paintings show nude youths with the word *kalos* above them—"a beauty." These practices are thought to have started in Sparta in the Iron Age and spread to Crete, then outward to all cities in the Mediterranean, and were certainly well established by 700 B.C. They are an integral part of ancient Greek culture.

SOCRATES

"THE UNEXAMINED LIFE is not worth living," said Socrates, who changed the field of philosophy. Earlier thinkers who lived in Asia Minor—what we now call the pre-Socratic philosophers—had just a few students. They focused primarily on explaining natural phenomena. Socrates, who lived from 470 to 399 B.C., focused on how humans best lived, and did not limit his teachings to a chosen few, but to anyone who would talk with him. According to his student Xenophon, "He was constantly in public, for he went in the morning to the places for walking and the gymnasia; at the time when the market was full he was to be seen there; and the rest of the day he was where he was likely to meet the greatest number of people; he was generally engaged in discourse, and all who pleased were at liberty to hear him."

From ancient texts, we learn the names of 300 people that Socrates talked with or knew through his social network—of all the ancient Greeks, he and Alexander the Great are the two about whom we have the most information. However, because Socrates never wrote down any of his ideas, all we know about him is secondhand. His student

DEATH OF SOCRATES: His friends visit him in prison.

Plato wrote the most, and it is hard to know which ideas are originally from Socrates and which are from Plato.

Socrates grew up poor and remained poor. His father was a stone-mason and sculptor, his mother a midwife. We don't exactly know how he earned money, but Plato emphasized that he never took a drachma for teaching philosophy. His friends and students adored him. His original mind questioned everything.

Early in Socrates' life, a friend went to Delphi and supposedly asked the oracle, "Who is the wisest person on earth?" and the answer was "Socrates." But Socrates modestly refused to believe it, saying only that he at least "knew what he did not know." He dedicated himself to finding a wiser man. To do that, he interviewed (some would say interrogated) everyone he met who seemed to have wisdom, even those he knew only by reputation.

Say a man was coming to court to make an accusation against someone. Socrates would ask him the meaning of justice, and begin a dialogue that would usually end in humiliation for the target—and giggles from the watching youths. As time went by, these youths began mimicking Socrates, accosting adults in their neighborhoods and talking in circles around them. Some parents probably found this behavior alarming. What made students love Socrates was his concern for their souls. Teaching, to Socrates, was about shaping the person to be the best he could be. He would talk of the "daimon" that sat on his shoulder and whispered advice when he had an ethical dilemma. That daimon was what we would call his conscience. There was no word for that in Greek or any earlier language. He invented or discovered the idea of having a conscience and living ethically based on its counsel.

Most people thought him an annoying oddball. He was brought up on charges of corrupting the youth by teaching them verbal gymnastics to belittle elders, and also a more serious charge of "importing new gods"—all this talk about daimons upset people. Behind these allegations were concerns that he was friends with some one-time leaders who had fallen out of favor. He was executed in 399 B.C., calmly drinking a shot glass of poison hemlock as his students looked on.

Socrates lived to be 70 years old, and by the end of his life he came around to believing there was nobody wiser. He said, "I am the wisest man alive, for I know one thing, and that is that I know nothing."

SOCRATES: Posthumous bust of the philosopher who transformed education and philosophy

ANAXIMANDER: Roman mosaic. The pre-Socratic philosopher holds a sundial.

PLATO'S ACADEMY
AND ARISTOTLE'S LYCEUM

SOCRATES TOOK GREEK PHILOSOPHY in an exciting new direction. But the original contribution of Socrates would have been insignificant had he not also been a gifted teacher, inspiring students to write about him and share his ideas with the world. His student Plato crafted a memory of Socrates that inspires students to this day. Through Plato's Academy, Socrates' teachings found an amplifier. A network of students and alumni expanded that influence.

Plato studied with Socrates and wrote many dialogues based on the conversations he heard. Plato also expressed his own views in works like *The Republic* and *The Laws*. Plato's student Aristotle expanded on his predecessors, writing all of his works in his own voice. Both Plato and Aristotle ultimately taught their students the most important thing of all, just in different ways: how to be a good person, pursue truth, and live a good life.

Plato institutionalized this Socratic school of philosophy in 387 B.C., a dozen years after the death of Socrates, by establishing his own school in the area of Athens called Academias. It was the first center for

LYCEUM OF ARISTOTLE: Excavations of site, discovered in 1996, where Aristotle and successors taught

advanced study for higher education. This is why universities are sometimes called "academies."

Before the fifth century, most people did not need to write. Lessons were learned through the spoken word and memorized. In his day, Plato would lament that his students had lost the ability to memorize because they relied too much on technology—writing on tablets!

Aristotle was a student at the Academy for 20 years, from age 17 to 37, and then took posts teaching in Sicily and Macedonia for more than a decade. He returned to Athens in 335 B.C. to establish his own university and placed it in the area of the city called the *lykeion*. We know it as the lyceum, and the French word for "high school," *lycée,* comes from this.

In both schools, learning was not based on lectures or courses. Instead, these were places where serious men went to have lively conversations, with well-known guests from other city-states popping in from time to time. No financial barriers prevented people from coming, and there were no strict dogmas to restrain original thinking. Over time a distinction developed between Plato's Academy and Aristotle's Lyceum. The Academy held that knowledge was generated through teaching, dialogue, and discussion. Aristotle felt new knowledge came through experimentation, research, collection of facts, observation, and classification. For this reason, he is known as the first scientist. The fault line between the humanities and the sciences started here.

Just as the sophists were hired to help youths acquire skills to become leading citizens, Plato, Aristotle, and their followers were hired by Greek kings. Plato served as court philosopher in residence in Syracuse, tutoring Dionysius II, who became king at a young age. A few years later, Plato returned to Athens to open his school. He wrote in *The Republic* that good city-states should be ruled by philosopher kings. He probably came to that conclusion after having a hard time stomaching that the inexperienced Dionysius II gained so much power so quickly. Aristotle was also hired as a tutor by a king, Philip II of Macedon, who wanted a good Greek education for his son, Alexander.

ARISTOTLE TUTORS ALEXANDER THE GREAT

HIPPOCRATES
AND HIS MEDICAL SCHOOL

HIPPOCRATES WAS A HEALER on the island of Kos around 500 B.C. He took careful notes on the progression of diseases in his patients, and recorded his treatments and the results. Writings from his successors make for gory but fascinating reading. Many of the ideas the Greek doctors developed about the way the organs work inside the body lasted until the 19th century.

Early medical knowledge also came from the battlefield. Ancient warfare involved spears, swords, and knives, all of which cut men open. The Greeks used bandages to close gaping wounds but also looked inside these gashes to understand the body better.

Physicians had more difficulty understanding the inside of women. They thought that the uterus moved inside a woman's body. When women became upset and emotional, that was the womb moving too high and pressing on her lungs to make her hyperventilate. The Greek word for uterus is *hysteros*—thus the diagnosis of hysteria. The cure was to coax the womb back down to its proper place. If one put something stinky at her mouth and nose, and something sweet smelling down below, that should take care of it.

Although doctors did not seem to know much about female anatomy, some women gained their own knowledge of health care. Mothers passed recipes for herbal remedies to their daughters. We think women developed these drugs through experimentation with flowers, crops, and berries during food preparation. Greek women also knew about birth control and abortifacients.

Health was thought to come from balance. The Greeks believed humans had four kinds of juices or vital fluids—black bile, yellow bile, blood, and phlegm—known as the four humors. Excess of any of these led to personality issues; black bile led to depression, for example. They also thought hot and cold, wet and dry needed to be in balance.

Sometimes there were catastrophic contagious diseases. At the beginning of the Peloponnesian War, Thucydides described a devastating plague in Athens. He recounts that people got such fevers that they stripped off their clothes and jumped into the public fountains. This probably didn't help! An estimated 75,000 people died. Thucydides says he caught the disease and survived. It killed Pericles, however.

ANCIENT MEDICINE: *(opposite)*
Achilles uses bandages to treat Patroclus's battle wounds.

HEALTH CARE CENTERS
OF ANCIENT GREECE

After Hippocrates died, his sons took over his medical practice, and those sons had sons, cousins, and nephews who all trained in medicine. Because what they knew was powerful, they controlled access to this knowledge, admitting only relatives into the field. The Hippocratic oath, still sworn today, outlines the principles of their trade. The doctors swore solidarity with other physicians, to first do no harm and to do good and avoid evil, not to assist in suicide or abortion, to leave surgery to surgeons, and not to seduce patients or make illegitimate house calls. They also swore to maintain confidentiality and never to gossip. This list gives an idea of how influential Greek medicine still is in contemporary society.

HEALING: A patient receives treatment from Asclepius and Hygieia.

ANATOMICAL OFFERINGS CORINTH: Gifts to Asclepius for healing

As the number of doctors grew and the field of medicine expanded, city-states set up special areas for sick people to receive treatment. They called them sanctuaries for Asclepius, god of healing. Asclepius in myth was the child of Apollo and a princess, Coronis. The princess died in labor and was laid out on a pyre to be cremated. Apollo rescued the child, performing the first C-section to cut Asclepius out from her womb. Because of this, Apollo is also a protector of health. Asclepius had two main helpers in myth and art. Hygieia is the goddess of health and the origin of our word "hygiene." She personifies health as a beautiful young woman, shiny and fresh, making everyone feel better. Panacea was a goddess who accompanied Asclepius in taking away the cares and worries of sick people. Release from daily stress and relief from pain are essential for healing, then and now.

The sanctuaries of Asclepius all over Greece had the usual temples, altars, theaters, and stadiums. But they also had the

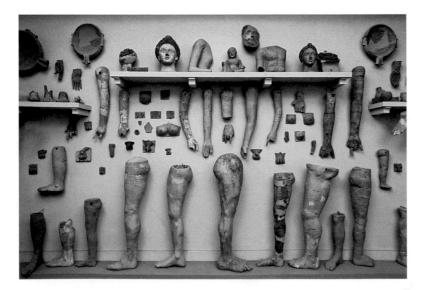

abaton, a hospital building with rooms for sleeping. Archaeologists have found surgical instruments in abatons. In the Hippocratic oath, physicians swear not to use the knife, but instead to turn cases over to specialists, the surgeons. At sanctuaries of Asclepius there were both physicians and surgeons. Archaeologists at many sanctuaries of Asclepius have found all sorts of medical instruments, including forceps, tweezers, hooks, scalpels, drills, knives, catheters, and even a speculum.

Patients at abatons would pray and leave offerings to the gods. At the Asclepius sanctuary in ancient Corinth, a great number of miniature and life-size clay body parts have been excavated. There are many eyes, noses, breasts, legs, arms, penises, and feet, most with a small hole up top for stringing a ribbon. We can imagine patients praying to Asclepius for that body part to be cured while hanging a likeness of it like a Christmas ornament on the wall of the temple. Patients would have hallucinations of snakes licking them and vivid dreams of blood. In the morning, they felt cured.

After a cure, patients would set up stone testimonials: "Wonder not at the greatness of this inscription but of the god, because he healed Cleo, after she had been pregnant and had carried the burden in her womb for five years, until she slept in the sanctuary." These primed the next patient to expect a successful outcome.

One of the most beautiful theaters in Greece is at the health center of Asclepius at Epidaurus. It is thought that patients would watch a play, and be transported back in time to the Age of Heroes. Aristotle believed that Greek tragedies produced catharsis, or purification, through the climactic scene. Such purification could prepare a patient for healing sleep in the abaton.

THEATER, EPIDAURUS: Near the best hospital in Greece, the stone theater seated 14,000 people.

CULTURAL CREATIVES

Most greeks made a living by farming, it is true. There were cottage industries, too, including products women made. Woven textiles, clay figurines, baked goods, cheeses, and yogurts made their way to market. But a surprisingly large number of the Greeks were craftsmen, including all sorts of artisans making beautiful things that weren't utilitarian. You can drink from any cup; why should it be meticulously painted? Who really needs all that jewelry? Why did they wear crowns and wreaths? What were the benefits of putting statues everywhere? None of this is necessary to survive or even to thrive. These people chose to live their lives immersed in beauty.

Marble sculptors experimented from the late seventh century B.C. with depicting the human form. At first the statues look rather stiff and awkward. Sculptures whose artists were from different Greek cities had slightly different looks. The stone nude males, called kouroi in the plural, look stocky and fleshy in Argos and Corinth, while the ones from Attica are slim. The ones made in Thebes have weird faces, with exaggerated smiles and big almond eyes. We aren't exactly sure if the kouroi represent a god, maybe Apollo, or a human, perhaps the one who dedicated it.

Some statues try to engage us in conversation: "Who are you and from where have you come? Klados is my name. Who raised you? Menophilus. Of what did you die? The fever. At what age? 13. Were you talented? Not really, the muses loved me not." An inscription on another statue is far less chatty: "I was not; I was; I shall be no more. It matters not to me."

The pervasive nudity of male figures on Greek vases and in sculpture is a bit puzzling for modern viewers. The artists were reflecting Greek culture, making objects that obviously sold in their market economy. It used to be said that this represented "heroic nudity," a kind of timeless idealization of the human form with universal appeal. These days a new interpretation is well accepted. The Greeks lived in an overtly bisexual world, where men were attracted both to other men and to women.

Male nudes were pleasurable and beautiful, and there was no stigma or shame in admiring them. But then shouldn't there be nude women, too, if the reason is sensual pleasure?

There aren't many nude depictions of women in vase painting, but they do exist. Ancient Greeks used a special shape of cup for drinking wine, as we do. Theirs, called a *kylix,* was like a soup bowl on a stem. Scenes were painted outside and inside. In one such scene, which appears in the circular interior (tondo), we see two women undressing for a bath, wrapping up their clothes, and bending to put them on stools. One is looking down, and the other is looking at the first over her shoulder. In other words, they don't know that they are being watched. When a man at dinner received this cup, it was filled with opaque red wine. He didn't know what was painted at the bottom. As he finished his red wine, tilting the bowl this way and that, the image would be revealed. Gulping down that last swallow, he would get to be a voyeur, seeing these women undressing, as if through a porthole. These kinds of amusing highbrow peep shows appear in many drinking cups.

TEMPLE OF HEPHAESTUS, ATHENS: Greece's best preserved temple is named for Hephaestus, who inspired metalsmiths and craftsmen.

PHIDIAS AND THE ACROPOLIS OF ATHENS

PARTHENON FRIEZE: Two riders; one wearing nothing but a cape

INTERIOR, PARTHENON: Kept inside were the cult statue of Athena Parthenos and dedications; Delian League funds may have been stored in its attic.

WHEN IT WAS INTACT, the Parthenon looked absolutely perfect, and that was because of minute imperfections. Each column has a unique curvature. Compare the rhythm of a metronome to a live human drummer. Because the drummer breathes, shifts, and moves, each beat is ever so slightly different. The Parthenon also has a pulse. It was made completely by hand.

In 454 B.C., there was no lockable gateway and no completed temple on the Acropolis, because the Persians had sacked it in 480 B.C. To protect the Delian League treasury, Pericles proposed an extensive building program, which included erecting the Parthenon and the gateway into the Acropolis, called the Propylaea. After vigorous debate in the Assembly, the citizens approved the entire ambitious project. Most urgent was to build the gateway to protect the treasury on the Acropolis. The next priority was a temple to protect Athena's treasures—the Parthenon.

The temple had 8 columns on the east and west sides and 17 on the long sides. Inside were two main rooms with shallow antechambers. The focal point was the cult statue of Athena, 36 feet tall, with ivory on her face and arms, and a ton of gold covering the drapery.

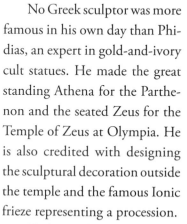

No Greek sculptor was more famous in his own day than Phidias, an expert in gold-and-ivory cult statues. He made the great standing Athena for the Parthenon and the seated Zeus for the Temple of Zeus at Olympia. He is also credited with designing the sculptural decoration outside the temple and the famous Ionic frieze representing a procession.

Phidias and Pericles became great friends. That became a problem. Rumor had it that Phidias had mishandled the gold for the drapery on the great statue of

THE TREASURES KEPT IN THE PARTHENON

ATHENA
PARTHENOS

AS ANCIENT VISITORS APPROACHED the Parthenon from the east, their view would have been very different from the wide-open marble floor that modern tourists see through two fields of columns. In those days, the inner six columns on the short ends of the temple had metal fences between them, effectively blocking the entry into the temple building or *cella*. Gold and silver items gleamed behind the fences. An elaborate door remained locked except for special occasions. When it opened, visitors could peer through to see the statue of Athena Parthenos.

Inside the main chamber with the cult statue were shelves, cupboards, and treasure chests filled with gold and silver vases and wreaths, plus statuettes, musical instruments, furniture, helmets, shields, and more. Just one of those gold bowls could have kept a trireme at sea for three months. Many dedications were inscribed with the name of the donor. Men tended to give gold wreaths, and women libation bowls and jewelry. Cities allied with Athens gave silver vases and gold wreaths, too.

The Parthenon was a visible savings account, assuring Athenians that they had cash if they needed it. At the end of the Peloponnesian War they became that desperate, and melted down much of Athena's treasures to fund the troops. In the fourth century they paid her back with interest.

Athena. Fortunately, on the advice of Pericles, he had designed the statue so that the gold could be taken off, weighed, and reassembled, like a giant kit. At trial, they weighed the gold, found it intact, and Phidias was found not guilty. Then someone noticed a striking resemblance between two figures carved on the statue's shield and the likenesses of Phidias and Pericles. This was blasphemy, and the Athenians brought Phidias back to court. In 430 B.C., he died in jail while the trial was ongoing, of grief or poison we will never know.

For 15 years, from 447 to 432 B.C., hundreds or even thousands of workers collaborated at the Acropolis. Quarrymen worked with the haulers, who needed suppliers of oxen, rope, and wood that arrived at the right times. Stonecutters needed tools, water, and even lunch. Working year after year in this way made for a very congenial and integrated lower class. Some slaves worked right beside them, earning the same wages. This unity would never again be seen, because of outbreak of the Peloponnesian War in 431 B.C.

ATHENIAN ACROPOLIS

ASCENDING THE ACROPOLIS is a breathtaking experience. Unless you are in shape, you really do feel breathless. At first you feel excited, and maybe walk too quickly. By the halfway mark, the calves tighten and breathing becomes heavy. Sweat drips. Your heart thumps. You feel mortal.

But then, climbing those last few steps, you enter the marble gateway, the Propylaea, standing in the disorienting shade, with a breeze like in a wind tunnel. Passing through the tall Ionic columns with their marble-coffered ceiling, you cross from shade into sunlight again and you are on the Acropolis plateau, the sacred ground. The Parthenon appears in three-quarter view. In antiquity, a 40-foot bronze statue of Athena made of melted armor from the Persian War would have been straight ahead of you. Like you, an ancient Athenian would have crossed, breathlessly, from the secular to the sacred worlds.

INVENTIONS OF THE GREEKS

MANY GREEK INVENTIONS, innovations, and discoveries have made lasting impacts on the world. The more obvious ones are democracy, voting, blind ballots, trial by jury, and constitutions. The Greeks also invented the theater and drama, both tragedies and comedies. They advanced the study of astronomy, learned from Babylonians, and predicted eclipses. They invented the genre of history, with Herodotus, then with Thucydides and beyond. The poets Homer and Hesiod were the authors of the earliest Western literature.

The Greeks developed hoplite warfare, which let them beat back the Persian invaders. For peacetime, they also invented many of the athletic competitions we know today: wrestling, boxing, javelin throw, discus, long jump, racing, and others. They invented the stadium with an oval track and a mechanical starting gate. Their classical style of architecture is still used in important public buildings. Greek medicine included surgery, herbs, and careful monitoring and observation. Greeks introduced the alphabet that Romans and Etruscans refined into the one we use now. They introduced minted coins to Europe. Philosophy. Higher education. So much more.

Even amid all that innovation, several inventors and inventions stand out.

Ctesibius, a third-century B.C. engineer, invented a pipe organ that used water instead of air. He improved the accuracy of water clocks used to keep time in public squares so much that his method remained popular until the 14th century, when lead weights and levers replaced the hydraulic mechanisms. Ctesibius invented the siphon and made great fountains. He put on amusing public shows with his contraptions. Among the highlights of his displays: a clay bird that sang, using pneumatic pressure on a tube with a counterweight. When the tube opened, air whistled melodiously through. He is to this day called the father of pneumatics.

Another inventor, Heron, made a vending machine. When a coin of the right weight dropped into a slot, a lever opened a lid that let holy water pour out of a pitcher. As the coin fell, it triggered another lever to close the lid back onto the pitcher, stopping the flow of water.

Mechanical inventions flourished in the fourth, third, and second centuries B.C. Robots, or automata, became a craze. The Greeks admired these self-moving carts (created using a complex sequence of

ANTIKYTHERA YOUTH: Life-size bronze statue of an unidentified hero or god, recovered from a shipwreck

releasing sand gradually over a weight and ropes), windup toys, and even cuckoo clock–style mini-theaters that put on tiny plays. Statues bobbled their heads; others appeared to be hammering by themselves. A third-century B.C. Greek working for the (Greek) Egyptian pharaoh Ptolemy II designed a plan to embed strong magnets from lodestones into a building, in order to suspend a life-size statue of the pharaoh's wife, making it look as if she were a floating goddess. That project wasn't realized, but the idea was later used in the Temple of Serapis in Alexandria, where an image of Amun the sun god hung in the air seemingly without support for 500 years, until the Romans closed all pagan sanctuaries in A.D. 391.

The most remarkable invention discovered in Greece was in a sunken ship found in 1900 by a sponge diver off the coast of the tiny island of Antikythera. Underwater archaeologists recovered 80 bronze parts that belonged to a machine, called the Antikythera mechanism. It has dials on the outside and 37 hand-cut gears of different sizes inside. Until 2006, no one knew what to make of it. Using three-dimensional x-ray scanners and high-resolution imaging, scientists read tiny lettering on the pieces. When the dials were turned, the machine could calculate eclipses and locate positions of the sun, moon, Venus, Mars, Mercury, and Saturn for any given day. The mysterious machine was an analog computer.

ANTIKYTHERA MECHANISM: An analog computer for calculating astronomy, a clocklike machine with 37 precise bronze gears

TECHNOLOGY IS BORN: PROMETHEUS GIVES FIRE TO HUMANS

IN GREEK MYTHOLOGY, the titan Prometheus was humanity's best friend. As the story goes, he created us in the form of gods out of water and clay. Over time, he felt sorry for us, because we lived in caves, labored with our bare hands, and shivered all night. Prometheus asked Zeus if he could give us fire and teach us to use it. With fire, humans could keep warm, smelt metal, cook food, build houses and ships, and eventually wage war. Zeus said no, out of fear we might get more power than we could handle. Prometheus went behind Zeus's back, hiding a flame in a hollow tube. When Zeus looked down one night and saw happy villagers warming themselves by the fire, he punished Prometheus by having him bound in chains to a distant rock, and sending a vulture to eat his liver every day for eternity. Eventually, the hero Hercules released him.

POP STARS AND CELEBRITIES: LYRIC POETRY

I N THE ARCHAIC AGE, beginning probably in the seventh century B.C., poets and musicians composed song lyrics that were so catchy that they spread throughout the Greek world. (The word "lyrics" comes from the Greek songs sung to the lyre.) From Sicily to Crete people sang about love, loss, desire, war, peace, aging, and friendship. Pindar's odes are a particular kind of poetry (called epinician) that celebrated individual athletes who won events at the games. The poems all have rhythms that would fit to music. Composed for feasts and festivals, these songs tended to be short and full of emotional impact.

Lyric poetry was usually written in the voice of the writer, first-person singular. The singer spoke from the heart. Earlier poems had been long epics, taking hours to perform, or hymns to the gods, with lofty language difficult for average people to learn or memorize. Shorter songs made the poet more popular and were easier for professional minstrels to add to their repertoire. This transition is captured in a poem by Anacreon from the mid-sixth century B.C.:

DOUBLE-FLUTE PLAYER: Cloaked musician entertains at a symposium; striped pillow and couch to left.

I, too, wish to sing of heroic deeds
(about the sons of Atreus, and about Cadmus),
but the lyre's strings
can only produce sounds of love.
Recently, I changed the strings,
and then the lyre itself,
and tried to sing of the feats of Hercules,
but still the lyre kept singing songs of love.
So, fare well, you heroes!
because my lyre sings only songs of love.

The poet Sappho wrote many beautiful lyric poems in the Archaic period, some so haunting that they resonate today:

THE MYTH OF THE INVENTION OF THE LYRE FROM A TORTOISESHELL

ZEUS LAY WITH MAIA in a mountain cave, to hide from Hera, his wife. At dawn Maia gave birth to a precocious infant, the god Hermes. An hour later the baby crawled out of the cave and saw a tortoise. Inspired, he cut the creature from its shell. He attached arms and a crosspiece, added strings of sheep gut, inventing the seven-string lyre, the first tuned instrument. By noon he was performing hymns.

The next time Hermes left the cave, he stole 50 of Apollo's cattle, walking them backward and wearing huge sandals to fool investigators. He crawled back to his crib, playing the innocent baby when Apollo came asking questions. Apollo had his suspicions, so he took Hermes to court. Zeus let the boy off. Apollo heard Hermes play the lyre and asked for it as compensation for the cattle. Hermes handed it over. That's how Apollo became the patron of music.

You may forget but
let me tell you
this: someone in
some future time
will think of us

APOLLO AND HIS LYRE: Roman wall painting shows the god of music and poetry.

The drinking song was also popular, and these tended to be very short, presumably repeated over and over by a group of men after way too much wine. In this example, the objects of desire are young boys rather than a lady. In ancient Greece, men had younger male lovers as well as wives and sometimes also went with paid dancers or flute girls who entertained at parties.

Would that I were a fine ivory lyre,
Struck by fair boys in Dionysus's choir.

And here is another drinking song:

I will choose a boy-loving life, that is far better than a wife;
Boyfriends in war a man can stand by, while the wife goes home to cry.

GIFTS TO THE GODS

THE GREEKS BELIEVED that the gods loved beautiful things, the shinier, the better. That is why Greek art is so beautiful, because most of it was made to be placed in sanctuaries as gifts to the gods. The larger, more famous sanctuaries held regular festivals and games. Winners commissioned inscriptions and statues of bronze and marble as thanks for their good fortune. When victors sacked a city, the fine things they took as loot were split among the soldiers, with a tithe given to a sanctuary. The temples were full of fine furnishings, ritual vessels and implements, and lots of gifts made of precious metals. Gold bowls, wreaths, and jewelry were most common, but few have survived the centuries.

Delphi received a great deal of dedications from city-states because of the oracle. Major civic decisions required a trip to Delphi, and the envoys would bring an expensive gift as payment. If things turned out well, they would send an offering of thanks, too. Many of the earliest dedications were intentionally buried when renovations took place after earthquakes, and so some of these treasures have been preserved. Archaeologists have discovered tremendous bronze cauldrons on tripod stands from the eighth century B.C. They also have found remains of several early gold-and-ivory statues, with well-preserved feet and golden hair.

Most of the bronze statues erected in sanctuaries have been lost—looted by later Greeks and Romans, hauled off to Constantinople, or melted down for weapons and armor. The stone statue bases remain, to show us where the figures once stood. Male or female marble statues could be gifts to the gods as well as grave markers. Bigger-than-life male marble statues were found at Cape Sounion in Attica as gifts to Poseidon, whereas marble females predominated on the Athenian Acropolis.

The Greek temples themselves also were gifts to the gods. With the sculpture from the Parthenon now available to be examined up close in

SPHINX, DELPHI: The people of Naxos dedicated to Apollo this marble sphinx atop a tall column.

the Acropolis and in the British Museum in London, we marvel that the statues that stood in the triangular areas of the short ends of the building were finished on both the front and back sides. These are sculptures in the round that stood on a high ledge and were attached to the building with dowels. They were 40 feet off the ground. No human would ever see the backs. And yet they are as beautifully carved as the front. Why? The sculptors wanted everything to be perfect. They were gifts to the gods.

Natural beauty was a criterion for situating a sanctuary for a god. Some locations had the power to move the visitor to tears, to make a worshipper gasp, or to fill people with awe. Some sit atop hills with breathtaking views. Some are in meadows where it is miraculously cool even in summer. The Greeks placed temples in spots where the cicadas are suddenly quiet, where there was a superabundance of chirping birds, or where the ambient noise of a babbling brook serenaded visitors. A place could sound unusual, feel colder or warmer than it should, or even smell more fragrant, as if a god were near. All the senses were involved in perceiving beauty. Walking through a forest, cutting through a field, or strolling on a beach, the devout noticed when conditions went from ordinary to extraordinary, or from average to beautiful, and they marked the spot.

There is a powerful scene in the play *Oedipus at Colonus,* where the writer Sophocles shows Oedipus, now blind and old, accompanied by his young daughter. Old Oedipus stops suddenly, and asks, "What is this place?" Antigone explains that they have just entered a sacred grove. He is blind, but he can feel the energy.

Beauty was a Greek ideal in life as well as in art. Both men and women were called "beauties," and songs praised male as well as female good looks. The male body was particularly admired when young and fit, captured in the surviving sculptures we see. In female statues, sculptors paid more attention to drapery and clothing than to the faces, which are usually generic. But beauty, as Plato wrote, is in the eye of the beholder, and a poem by Sappho, a female poet from Lesbos, demonstrates that:

> Some say a host of horsemen, others of infantry,
> And others of ships, is the most beautiful thing
> On the black earth; but I say, it is whom you love.

WINGED VICTORY OF SAMOTHRACE: Commemorating a victory in a sea battle, Nike alights on the ship's prow.

GREEK TEMPLES: VARIATIONS ON A THEME

ARCHAIC AND CLASSICAL GREEK temples were always rectangular boxes. Columns march around the outside. Inside there is a walled room or two, occasionally three. The temples sit on a three-stepped platform.

There were three types of Greek temples. The first is the Doric order, where the columns sit flat on the floor with no base. The top is a simple capital, looking like a pillow where the column meets what is called the entablature, the horizontal parts that support the pitched roof. Doric columns are fluted with sharp ridges at the peaks. In the Doric order, the entablature includes the Doric frieze, a horizontal band adorned by a series of plaques, called metopes, divided by blocks of three vertical stripes, called triglyphs.

The Ionic order has ring-shaped column bases, taller columns with tongue depressor–like flutes and flat peaks, and column capitals shaped like two scrolls. Ionic buildings have a different frieze, consisting of

SELINUNTE, SICILY: All Greek city-states built temples with a walled inner sanctum surrounded by a colonnade.

HOW DID THEY MOVE THOSE STONES?

ONCE QUARRIED, STONES had to be transported to the construction site. Usually stones were hauled on ox-drawn sleds that rolled on logs. As the sled moved forward, it rolled off the back log, which men would bring around to the front. This could go on for miles. To get the sled up a hill, laborers dug pegs in along the side of the road, and strung ropes from the cart up and around the peg for leverage. Then everyone would line up on both sides and pull. The cart would inch uphill. They would pull the rope again. It was hard work, with some stones weighing ten tons. Once the stones reached the work site, wooden cranes with pulleys were used to lift them. Men built scaffolding to get the stones into place at the top of the buildings. This was dangerous work, but only one man that we know of died working on the Acropolis buildings during those 15 years.

three flat ribbons, on top of which is a wider ribbon, sometimes carved with figures. The ornate Corinthian order, introduced in the late fifth century, has tall proportions like the Ionic, but the elaborate capitals look like layers of bent leaves.

Within those three types, each temple is unique because of its size, its materials, its exterior decorations, and the proportion, spacing, and shape of its columns. Some are limestone, others are marble, and the metopes in the Peloponnese were sometimes clay plaques. Limestone blocks could be painted with marble dust to look like marble, as at the great Temple of Zeus at Olympia. All temples took money, time, and labor to build. They were built to last for all time, and many have.

Because Greece has many earthquakes, temples were built without mortar or other adhesive to keep the stones together. Columns can be made of one enormous piece of stone, but were usually made by stacking cylinders on top of each other. The stairs, floors, and entablature were kept together with clamps. There was just enough flexibility to withstand tremors. Some temples didn't make it, and were rebuilt. There were at least three temples on the spot of the oracle at Delphi, the first destroyed by fire, the second by earthquake, and the third again by fire. The Temple of Artemis at Ephesus, one of the seven wonders of the ancient world for its enormous size, was destroyed by fire on the night that Alexander the Great was born. Some people took that as an auspicious sign, but others as just a coincidence.

WOMEN'S FASHIONS

WHEN A WOMAN MARRIED, her father would give the groom a dowry. If the couple separated, she could keep her clothes and jewelry. So women would collect jewelry when they could. In a comedy written by Aristophanes, *Thesmophoriazusae,* an actor lists the items a woman might have that reads like the contents of a modern purse: "an earring, a piece of gemstone-studded gold, earrings, a necklace, a grape cluster pendant, headbands, broaches, bracelets, collars, anklets, seals, chains, rings, mold-made beads, hollow beads, bands, dildos, items from Sardis, necklaces, hoop earrings, and a whole bunch of stuff you would be hard pressed to name."

A woman's clothing varied from rough wool to fine linen. The simplest garment was a peplos, made of a rectangle like a sheet. Try peplos origami with a piece of paper. Fold it in half with the two short ends together. Turn it so that the folded edge is at the top. Move your fingers down about an inch or so from that top edge and fold so the top flops over itself. To close the garment, fold this in half, making sure that the flap is on the outside. Now wrap it around a lady like a towel, except over her shoulders, not under her armpits. Wait a minute: One side is still open! (A belt will take care of that.) Long metal pins with knobs pinch the peplos closed on both shoulders around the woman's head. Her arms would poke through both edges—the fabric is softer than our piece of paper. Fancier linen chitons had an embroidered stripe, worn over a thin, crinkly slip. Both men and women wore wool capes called himations.

Women spent a lot of time washing clothes, in rivers, lakes, or washbasins. They fetched water from public fountains, which served as social clubs. They could also socialize at religious festivals and sanctuaries. At night they held their own parties while the men went out to symposia, although some husbands would lock their wives at home in the evenings.

Unmarried adult women could have lovers who gave them presents and places to live. Writers refer to them as hetaerae, "companions," formerly translated as harlots or prostitutes. But modern shaming just doesn't apply in ancient Greece. When Pericles left his wife, he took up with Aspasia, a woman from a reputable foreign family who was his intellectual equal. It is said that they kissed in public and were partners for the rest of his life. Socrates said all Pericles' best ideas came from her.

CARYATIDS: *(opposite)* The porch of the maidens called caryatids is part of the Erechtheion on the Acropolis.

THE FIRES OF HEPHAESTUS: GREEK METALWORK

BRONZE GOD: This life-size bearded god, interpreted as Zeus or Poseidon, aims his thunderbolt or trident.

ANTIKYTHERA YOUTH, DETAIL: Eyes are inlaid with stone and white glass paste for realistic effect.

METALSMITHS MADE GREAVES and breastplates that were anatomically correct from at least the seventh century B.C. Greaves had calf muscles; breastplates had pectorals, abdominals, and sometimes nipples. So for metalsmiths to move from making bronze armor to statues was perhaps not such a stretch.

The surviving full-size bronze statues, mainly of nude males, look quite realistic. The lips and nipples are made of copper. The bronze eye sockets were holes, in which stones were inset to look like real eyes, with bronze eyelashes. The term "bionic" comes to mind. Ancient authors who wrote about them found them superhuman and awe inspiring.

The statues pose in mid-action: tying a hair ribbon, holding out an apple, or about to hurl a spear. We call this the classical moment, when an artist represents a figure just as he is about to do something or just after doing something, but not at the height of the action. This leaves the viewer room for imagination.

Metalsmiths also made practical objects, such as drinking cups, pitchers, and bowls, sometimes of silver or gold. These were decorated with all kinds of attachments, including griffons, gods, the Medusa, animals, grapes, leaves, or birds. The intricacy of the silver found in the tomb of Philip II at Vergina must be imagined all over Greece, especially in the late fifth century B.C. and later.

Inventory lists of temple treasures record large silver water jugs, made at a standard weight and acting as a kind of bullion. Golden figurines of the goddess of victory, Nike, also were basically made as gold bars. One metalsmith, Nicocrates of Colonus, was commissioned by the Athenian treasurers to melt down gold jewelry and smaller cups to consolidate into these larger shapes. Between 334 and 311 B.C. he made 26 such vessels. He would take broken necklaces, earrings missing a mate, small silver vases that didn't stack well and cluttered up the place. These were melted and refashioned into vases that could be used in religious ceremonies and weighed roughly the same as each other.

Sometimes conquerors melted down silver and gold statues of the defeated. Sometimes internal rebellions led to melting down other statues. In one case, when an odious dictator named Demetrius of Phalerum was deposed, 300 portrait statues of his were melted, we are told. Some of that metal was used to make chamber pots.

The bronze statues that survive have been found mainly in underwater excavations. Usually some Roman ship sank, carrying off Greek statues to Italy. The most famous Greek bronzes include the Apoxyomenos of Croatia, found in 1999; the Delphi Charioteer; the Artemision god Zeus (or maybe Poseidon); the horse and jockey, also of Cape Artemision; the Piraeus Poseidon and Athena; the two warriors called the Riace bronzes; and the Antikythera youth.

In 2013, a Palestinian fisherman in Gaza claimed to have discovered a submerged life-size bronze statue of Apollo, seven feet tall. He dragged it home, cut off a finger, and melted it to see what it was made of. When photos were released of it, scholars identified it as a bronze kouros in the Archaic style. In the photos, the statue was lying on a sleeping bag decorated with blue Smurfs, and it was briefly posted on eBay for $500,000. It hasn't been seen since.

DERVENI BRONZE CRATER: Large ornamented bowl for wine from a tomb near Thessaloniki

NEXT STOP: ANCIENT GOLD WREATHS

THESSALONIKI IS THE SECOND largest city in Greece, founded in 315 B.C. and named after Alexander the Great's half sister. Located near Pella and Aigai, the Macedonian capitals, the area would have been well populated in antiquity, which means generations of people lived and died there. When the city decided to build a 21st-century subway system, builders excavated down to ancient levels. They were careful, and had archaeologists on staff. In 2009, a year after subway digging began, the crews hit an ancient cemetery, recovering eight gold wreaths from the graves. A ninth gold wreath was found in 2013, this time on a man whose skeleton was entirely preserved. More than 28,000 ancient and medieval artifacts reportedly have been recovered so far, and they aren't done yet. When Athens built its subway for the 2004 Olympics, they found 30,000 artifacts.

MACEDONIAN GOLD WREATH

THE LAWS OF ALL MEN

STATUE OF THEMIS: The goddess, who personified the concept of justice, enforced treaties.

THE GREEK GODDESS THEMIS, also known as goddess of good counsel, embodied justice. In mythology, she alone of all the gods and goddesses stands for ethical conduct. She never lies, cheats, steals, or commits adultery the way most of the others do. She was one of the earliest wives of Zeus, who also guaranteed punishment for lawbreakers.

She supervised fair treatment of adversaries in the law courts and on the battlefield, where she oversaw the rules of warfare. The Greeks called these unwritten but commonly accepted rules "the laws of all men." The laws, for example, protected prisoners of war and allowed the vanquished to retrieve bodies from the battlefield and to bury their dead.

Wars ended with treaties, which Themis guaranteed. When laws or treaties were violated, that was cause for war. When leaders of city-states stole from temples or used temple land for commercial gain, that was cause for war. When city-states broke treaties by attack, that was also cause for war.

Some Greeks committed war crimes, such as executing prisoners of war and massacring noncombatants. But Greek society found such acts abhorrent. When judging these crimes from a modern perspective, we have to remind ourselves how brutal war was then. There was no Geneva Convention, no threat of trials in The Hague. Assyrians chopped off noses. Persians mastered the art of torture. At one point, the men of Corinth wanted to chop off Athenians' arms, but the Spartans wouldn't let them. It was standard practice to enslave whole populations and sell them or bring them to the land of the victors.

Uniquely, the Greeks developed a code of behavior among themselves about negotiating treaties and letting the defeated go home when the battle ended. Sometimes the men were still massacred and the women and children enslaved, but that was not the norm.

The Peloponnesian Wars actually were two conflicts between the Athenian Empire and Sparta and its allies, known as the Peloponnesian League. The first phase, from 431 to 421 B.C., was triggered when Athens violated traditions that allowed colonies to remain allied with their mother-cities. Athens tried to force Potidaea, a Corinthian colony in northern Greece, to join the Delian League. Athens also interfered in domestic affairs in Epidamnus, a colony of Corfu and Corinth, allies of Sparta. These acts alone would not have started a war with Sparta had it not been for the growing anxiety over Athens's wealth and power after 50 years at the helm of the Delian League.

During these years, the two adversaries fought on battlefields but also raided each other's territories, taking their aggressions out on farmers' fields, vines, and fruit trees as often as on human beings. They sailed to ports belonging to the enemy alliance, threatening them and trying to win them over. Peace came only when the generals of both sides were killed at the Battle of Amphipolis in 421 B.C.

A treaty called the Peace of Nicias that was meant to last for 50 years broke in just 5, when Athens in 416 B.C. tried to make Melos, a tiny island that had been neutral, join the Delian League or be destroyed. The chilling description by Thucydides of the debate between the Melians and the Athenian envoys includes the argument that might makes right, spoken from the Athenian side:

ZEUS: Greeks believed Zeus, top center, stood ready with thunderbolt to smite wrongdoers and criminals.

> *For of the Gods we believe, and of men we know, that by a law of their nature wherever they can rule they will. This law was not made by us, and we are not the first who have acted upon it; we did but inherit it, and shall bequeath it to all time, and we know that you and all mankind, if you were as strong as we are, would do as we do.*

The Melians begged Athens to let them remain neutral, and refused to submit. The men were all put to death, and every single woman and child was sold into slavery.

CRIMINAL JUSTICE IN ATHENS

THE GREEKS INVENTED LAW courts and trials; in the earlier Near Eastern civilizations, people generally were brought before a king or small circle of oligarchs and summarily executed, fined, tortured, or let go. Having a law code in a public place meant people could get equal treatment before the law. They called this *isonomia,* and it was a slogan for freedom and rights when citizens made democratic revolutions.

It was important to punish wrongdoers in court, but the Greeks believed they would be punished by the gods, regardless. The main aim of the courts was to protect the city from the pollution of harboring a criminal. Sophocles says it best in *Antigone:* "When he honors the laws of the land and the gods' sworn right, high indeed is his city; but stateless the man who dares to dwell with dishonor."

Many ancient Greek laws sound oddly contemporary, dealing with the consequences for the same crimes and civil issues that we face. That is because when people live in cities, the same kinds of problems come up, no matter the era. Here is a law from the Cretan town of Gortyn, written in the fifth century B.C. It sounds like a modern U.S. statute: "If a husband and wife be divorced, she shall have her own property

AGORA, ATHENS: As it looked in Roman times, with classical buildings far right

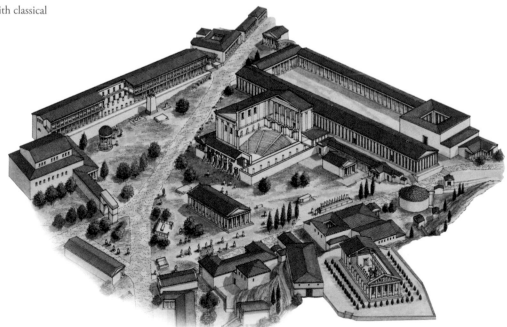

that she came with to her husband, and the half of the income if it be from her own property, and whatever she has woven, the half, whatever it may be, . . . if her husband be the cause of her dismissal; but if the husband deny that he was the cause, the judge shall decide."

Sometimes families were torn apart by civil wars and women bore the brunt of it. In myth, Antigone was the daughter of Oedipus; her brothers were on opposite sides of a civil war in Thebes. The king, Creon, honored one but decreed that the other must remain unburied. Antigone had to decide whether to follow the city's law or the laws of Themis. She chose heaven with these words from Sophocles' play *Antigone*: "Yes; for it was not Zeus that had published me that edict; not such are the laws set among men by the justice who dwells with the gods below; nor deemed I that thy decrees were of such force, that a mortal could override the unwritten and unfailing statutes of heaven. For their life is not of today or yesterday, but from all time, and no man knows when they were first put forth." From time immemorial, girls had buried the dead in their families, so she defied the king.

THE RIGHT TO A SPEEDY TRIAL

WATER CLOCK

ATHENS DEVELOPED AN EFFICIENT process for jury trials. People could come to the chief magistrates, known as archons, and make accusations. The accused person would come forth and a trial would begin, facilitated by a magistrate, but without police or judges. Each party would speak and call witnesses. Juries would debate and decide. Penalties ranged from fines to exile, with the rare death penalty, as Socrates received.

In classical Athens, no lawyers existed yet. Each person prosecuted or defended by himself. Once the jury was selected, the trial began immediately. A water clock kept time. The clock consisted of two jars of the same size, one placed on a block for elevation. When it was time for a speech, a plug would be pulled from the base of the first jar. Water poured out into the second jar. When the top jar ran dry, the speech was over.

The Greeks also invented the blind ballot. Each juror got two bronze tops, one with a hollow spindle (guilty), and the other solid (innocent). When they were held between a thumb and finger, no one could see which was which. Each juror dropped his vote in a box, and his discard in another.

THE GREEK AFTERLIFE AND THE ELEUSINIAN MYSTERIES

I N THE COURSE OF DAILY LIFE, people feared the gods would punish them for cheating someone or violating rules of hospitality. The poet Hesiod warned of the consequences: "There is a noise when Justice [Themis] is being dragged in the street where those who devour bribes and give sentence with crooked judgements, take her. And she, wrapped in mist, follows to the city and haunts of the people, weeping, and bringing mischief to men, even to such as have driven her forth in that they did not deal straightly with her."

Civil behavior in Greek society was enforced by the common belief in the afterlife. Many Greek myths explored themes of eternal punishment. Tantalus was sentenced to eternal thirst, with a cup of water just out of reach—a sentence that is the source of our word "tantalize." Sisyphus was doomed to push a heavy rock up a hill, only to have it roll down so he has to start over.

Hades was lord of the underworld in Greek myth. Most people who go down to his realm remain there, but a few heroes visited this place and returned to tell of it. Among them was Orpheus, son of a Muse, blessed with a great voice and musical talent. Animals in the forest would stop whatever they were doing and listen to him play the lyre. He attracted many women, but spurned them all until Eurydice came into his life. They fell madly in love. One day, they went for a picnic, and a snake bit her foot. She died. Orpheus couldn't stop thinking about her, and his sad songs drove all who heard him to tears. Finally he went to Hades, and demanded his bride back. Hades agreed to allow him to bring her out of his kingdom, but only on the condition that she would follow him up the stairs and he could not look at her until they got to the sunlight. Overjoyed, he agreed. He started up the stairs, heard her familiar footsteps behind, and then, it sounded like she slipped. Instinctively, he turned to help her up, he saw her, and she disappeared.

MYSTERIES AT ELEUSIS: Ceramic plaque depicts elements of the ceremonies; mid-fourth century B.C.

Everyone was judged by Hades, whose palace was guarded by the triple-headed dog, Cerberus. After judgment, if they had lived a good life and were remembered by the living, they could stay in the fields of

Asphodel, and if they were really deserving, move on to the Elysian Fields. Tartarus and its dark pits were for those who violated the laws of society. Only the forgotten and unburied wandered around on the banks of the Styx, unable to cross over to the House of Hades for all eternity.

The agricultural goddess Demeter, whose daughter Persephone lived with Hades half the year, was worshipped in part because the Greeks believed that crops failed when the city was polluted by wrong-doing. An ancient hymn to Demeter says, "Then she went, and to the kings who deal justice . . . she showed the conduct of her rites and taught them all her mysteries . . . Happy is he among men upon earth who has seen these mysteries; but he who is uninitiated and who has no part in them, never has good things once he is dead, down in the darkness and gloom."

In the town of Eleusis, west of Athens, archaeologists uncovered altars and temple buildings going back to the Bronze Age. The classical sanctuary was the most important cult center to Demeter and the heart of the "Eleusinian Mysteries." It had a huge square auditorium with a large stone box in the middle. The initiation ceremonies had something to do with secret "things done, seen, and heard," emanating from the box. Once initiated, Demeter's followers believed that they were saved. The rites continued until the late fourth century A.D. In all that time, no writer ever revealed the secrets that came from the box.

ELEUSIS RELIEF: Demeter, left, and Persephone, right, with youth Triptolemus, inventor of the plow

THE ORIGINS OF FRATERNITIES AND SORORITIES

ON COLLEGE CAMPUSES, many students join Greek letter organizations—fraternities and sororities. The first Greek letter fraternity, Phi Beta Kappa, started at the College of William & Mary in Williamsburg, Virginia, in 1776. Greek and Latin were required languages for college students, who became fascinated with Demeter's religious cult. The traditional stages of initiation—pledge week, hazing, secrecy, and more—all derive from what these students studied in their classics courses. The ancient ceremonies lasted nine days and involved drinking a lot of mint beer, then walking from Athens to Eleusis. Along the way, people dressed as trolls popped out of bushes and from under a bridge to taunt the initiates. There was much purification, ritual washing, and prayer. Finally, worshippers received a secret revelation. In modern times, there may be less purification and more beer, but the atmospherics remain similar, binding members together through communal heightened experiences.

DELPHI

ZEUS RELEASED TWO EAGLES, East and West, to locate the middle of the Earth's surface. Both landed at Delphi, from then on considered the navel of the universe. Delphi, where two subterranean fault lines intersect, is indeed an extraordinary place, with its dramatic mountain landscape and unusually cool temperatures. The Castalian Spring provides sweet, fresh water. Greeks conserved such special places by calling them sanctuaries and marking the territory as sacred.

Delphi became rich, not just because pilgrims came for prophecies but also because one of the Panhellenic festivals, the Pythian Games, took place there every four years. The games included track-and-field sports for men, as well as music contests in which women could compete. On the first day, the opening ceremonies featured a reenactment of Apollo slaying a snake called Pytho. Some think that this was the origin of Greek drama.

ASK THE ORACLE

APOLLO WAS THE MOST cerebral of the Greek gods, associated with healing, sunlight, music, and above all, prophecy and oracles. In ancient times, people believed the gods sent signs. Flight patterns of birds, or strikes of lightning, or the color of newborn animals could all have meaning. Augury involved examining the livers of sacrificed animals to read the signs. We might call this superstition, but when a community needed guidance in making important decisions, these signs legitimized the choices, ensuring stability and unity in the face of a challenge. Many Greek city-states sent ambassadors to Delphi when they were struggling, and the oracle would advise them about what to do.

The oracle at Delphi has a long pedigree, with evidence that people came there in the Bronze Age, when the area was sacred to Gaea, Mother Earth. The Temple of Apollo stood on Mount Parnassus, with one of the most beautiful vistas in Greece. Tradition says a goatherd was the first person to discover Delphi's prophetic powers. He noticed that when his animals approached the spot, their voices changed and then they all jumped into a crevice in the rock. He told the villagers, who placed a tripod stool there, and sat a young woman on it. She then spoke in tongues. One day a stranger on horseback grabbed her and rode off. The villagers replaced her with an old woman who would not be stolen away. The Pythia, as she was called, received prophecies from Apollo, slayer of the snake Pytho. Priests would translate her gibberish for worshippers. People came from all over to receive these prophecies, which were often open to multiple interpretations.

TEMPLE OF APOLLO, DIDYMA:
The forest of Ionic columns and the temple's blinding white marble enhanced the oracle's mystique.

What made her speak in tongues? A very solid temple has stood at Delphi since the Archaic period. In 2001, scientists found that two faults intersect on this spot, and potentially hallucinogenic ethylene gas comes through the fractures. Traditionally, the Pythia held forth with her prophecies from an inner chamber under the temple. It's easy to see how someone, particularly with the weight of social expectations, could spout oracles in that confined, gas-filled space.

There were other famous centers for prophecy. At Dodona in Epiros in northwestern Greece, unwashed, barefoot priests and aged priestesses interpreted the rustling of the branches and leaves of an ancient oak tree. Zeus was the main god there, not Apollo. "For these are the priests; and one is charged with hanging the garlands, one with uttering the prayers, a third must attend to the sacrificial cakes, and another to the barley-grains and the basket, another makes a sacrifice, and another will permit no one else to flay the victim," wrote Philostratus the Elder.

The oracle of Zeus at the Siwa Oasis was a weird Greek oracle in the Libyan Desert that had priests who walked on a giant checkerboard carrying a canoe. They weaved and wobbled, moving this way and that, as a scribe recorded their path. It was like a Ouija board, and the prophecies were interpretations drawn from where the priests walked. Alexander the Great went there to ask if he was destined to conquer the Persian Empire. All we know is that he was told what he wanted to hear.

TEMPLE OF APOLLO, DIDYMA, DETAIL: Medusa's deeply carved curls, eyes, and lips create menacing shadows.

THE ORACLE AT DIDYMA AND ALEXANDER THE GREAT

A NATURAL SPRING gave Apollo's oracle at Didyma its prophetic powers. Located in Asia Minor near Miletus, it has some of the most impressive marble architectural remains ever found, and was the fourth largest temple in the Greek world—but the temple was never finished. The podium is hollow, with paths and chambers for priests to scurry around while the oracle's theatrics took place up top. The columns were seven feet in diameter, and there were 122 of them. The walls rose more than 80 feet high. The scale of it stirred fear and awe. It inclined most people to believe what the oracle said.

Most of it remained open to the air, with just a small inner building to protect and contain the cult statue of Apollo. Because Didyma was a Greek settlement, the Persians sacked it in 479 B.C. in the Persian Wars. It is said that the sacred spring stopped flowing at that moment and the oracle went mute, until Alexander the Great, who regularly consulted oracles, came through in 331 B.C.. He sought a prediction regarding his plans to conquer the Persian Empire. Miraculously, this reestablished the spring and oracle of Apollo at Didyma, which announced that Alexander was the son of Zeus and not Philip, and that he would triumph. Alexander got the prophecy that he came for.

LET'S GET TOGETHER

AKEY TO THE CREATIVITY and innovation inherent in ancient Greece was having plenty of face time. There were 1,000 city-states, many with only the population of a small town. Even in larger ones, where no one could know everyone else, there were many chances to mix and mingle. As one anonymously written drinking song had it:

> Drink with me, and sport with me,
> Love with me, wear crowns with me,
> Be mad with me when I am moved with rage,
> And modest when I yield to counsels sage.

The Greeks had holidays and festivals far more often than we do, and at these they marched, paraded, sacrificed, competed, sang, and ate in different clusters, moving from one to the next so that they met as many people as possible. This happened throughout the year, so the odds improved that everyone in the city-state was three hops or fewer from knowing everyone else. Tight-knit "small worlds" make it easier for networks to efficiently spread information, news, and ideas. Just think how quickly gossip can move through a small town.

When the little germs of the city-states consisted of just a few related families, huddled together in the forest inside their wood huts, farming, hunting, and gathering, the men gathered nightly to sit by a fire, tell stories, sing songs, and drink wine. These gatherings promoted harmony, egalitarianism, and cooperation.

When the Greek Renaissance opened the door to trade and travel after 750 B.C., followed by colonization, people interacted more often with others from outside their village. A host offered anyone who came to the door a bath, a meal, and something to drink. Only then would he ask who the visitors were and what business they had there. Some

WINE CRATER: Animals brought for sacrifice to Delphi, with altar, tripod, and temple, right

Greeks believed that gods came disguised as mortals, as they do in Homer's epics, and so strangers should be treated well.

Banquets with entertainment, plenty of food, and wine figure prominently in Homer's narratives, and by the seventh century, the Greeks were emulating their heroes with elaborate banquets of their own. By the sixth century, wealthy Greeks were partaking in nightly dinner parties in cities throughout the Greek world, visiting each other's homes and hosting friends. The ritual was known as a "symposium," a word that literally means "drinking together." Symposia became the engines of innovation in the development and spread of new ideas. These were opportunities for elite and educated men to affirm and strengthen a network of private relationships that would help them in business and civic life, like clubs do for a certain set today.

Aristotle famously wrote, "Man is a political animal." This had nothing to do with election campaigns. Rather, the word "political" comes from polis, the "city-state." Aristotle was saying that humans are made for living in cities; we reach our maximum potential when we collaborate with fellow citizens.

PARTHENON FRIEZE, DETAIL: Procession of two males and a female carrying water jars up to the Acropolis

SYMPOSIA: GREEK PARTY LIFE

WHAT A WAY TO GO. The bones of the fellow buried in the Tomb of the Diver from Paestum in southern Italy were surrounded on all four walls by painted frescoes of a symposium. One man reclines on a cushioned couch, in the company of men dressed in fine linen. Painted tables hold bread, olives, and other savory snacks. In such settings, the host would salute Dionysus, Zeus, and the peculiar, enigmatically named "Good God" with a prayer; then the drinking begins. Wine pours freely from a large ceramic punch bowl in the middle. Youthful servants, good-looking and lithe, keep the cups filled. Fragrant incense burns; ornate carpets and tapestries cover stone floors and walls. Lamplights and torches flicker. All the senses are engaged. The body feels pleasure, and the mind is alive. This was a particularly Greek kind of heaven—an everlasting symposium, a leisurely dinner party where men ate, drank, and talked together.

Aristophanes, in his comedy *The Wasps,* exaggerated but also accentuated the emphasis on aesthetics in the tradition of the symposium:

> — *Come and lie down, and learn how to be a symposiast and*
> *a socialite.*
> — *How do I lie, then? Come on, tell me.*
> — *Elegantly.*
> —*You want me to lie like this?*
> — *Oh no.*
> — *How then?*
> — *Straighten your knees and pour yourself over the cushions,*
> *limply and athletically. Then praise the bronzes, inspect the*
> *ceiling, admire the hangings on the wall.*

Amid the seeming frivolity, one pleasure at the symposium might surprise us: the enjoyment that came from serious conversation. Plato and Xenophon recorded such conversations, and many others mentioned them. Inspired by Dionysus' wine, the men commenced discussions on the true nature of things. As each attendee offered a speech, song, poem, or story, the subject came into sharper view. The rich aesthetic context heightened the senses while expanding and challenging the mind.

TOMB OF THE DIVER, PAESTUM:
(opposite) An eternal symposium decorated this man's grave.

AT THE TABLE WITH SOCRATES

TASTE A DINNER CONVERSATION between Socrates and a brilliant woman, probably fictional, Diotima of Mantinea:

"When a man loves the beautiful, what does he desire?" I answered her, "That the beautiful may be his." "Still," she said, "the answer suggests a further question: What is given by the possession of beauty?" . . . I replied, "I have no answer ready." "Then," she said, "let me put the word 'good' in the place of the beautiful, and repeat the question . . . If he who loves, loves the good, what is it then that he loves?" "The possession of the good," I said. "And what does he gain who possesses the good?" "Happiness," I replied; "there is less difficulty in answering that question." "Yes," she said, "the happy are made happy by the acquisition of good things. Nor is there any need to ask why a man desires happiness; the answer is already final." "You are right," I said.

DIONYSUS: GOD OF WINE AND CREATIVITY

A S PROMETHEUS HELPED humanity by giving us technology, so the Greeks looked at Dionysus as their benefactor for his gift of wine. They saw Dionysus as a god with a dual nature, who inspired ecstasy and heightened consciousness, and also rage and violent revenge, reflecting alcohol's effects. His followers in myth were satyrs and maenads. Satyrs represented the baser, drunken state of males, who behave as beasts and cannot control themselves. The female maenads had wild wavy hair, and held a wand called the thyrsus that looks like an artichoke on a pike. They were said to catch wild rabbits by the ears, suckle fawns, and rip cattle apart with their bare hands.

When people think of Greek orgies, or call them "bacchanals," they are talking about female maenads cavorting with male satyrs in myth and Dionysus worshippers in real life. Dripping with ivy and waving their artichoke wands, they indeed did some crazy things, and would leave city life for a few days to revel. Women were allowed to join in, which must have felt quite liberating.

DIONYSUS: *(opposite)* Vase detail shows the god wearing a leopard skin and ivy wreath with grape vines in the background.

A SCENE FROM *THE BACCHAE,* BY EURIPIDES

BACCHAE

A SPY REPORTS to the king of Thebes what he saw:

> There beneath the trees sleeping they lay, like wild things flung at ease in the forest . . . Then rose the Queen Agâvê suddenly amidst her band, and gave the god's wild cry, "Wake up, Bacchae! I hear the sound of horned cattle. Awake!"—Then, all around, alert, the warm sleep fallen from their eyes, a marvel of swift ranks I saw them rise, women young and old . . . And one a young fawn held, and one a wild wolf cub, and fed them with white milk, and smiled in love . . . And one would raise her wand and strike the rock, and straight a jet of quick bright water came. Another set her thyrsus in the bosomed earth, and there was red wine that the God sent up to her . . . O King, had you been there, as I, and seen this thing, with prayer and most high wonder would you commence to adore this god whom now you rail against!"

TRAGEDIES AND COMEDIES

Unlike today, plays in ancient times were not just for entertainment. The Greek tragedies were performed in the context of the festival of Dionysus, held in March when the vines began to come back to life. Although we know the most about the festival of Dionysus in Athens, approximately 90 ancient theaters have been excavated so far in the Greek world, including in Sicily, Italy, Macedonia, Cyprus, and Asia Minor.

At the main festival in Athens, each competing playwright produced three plays. Two were tragedies and one was a short satyr play—raunchy skits featuring costumed satyrs, the drunken revelers associated with Dionysus.

The tragedies could not be more different from the satyr plays. Tragedies explore love, loss, free will, guilt, the abuse of power, and pride (or hubris). Typically the star commits a terrible crime or makes a move without realizing how foolish and arrogant he has been. The chorus lets the audience know what is coming. As the protagonist slowly realizes his error, his world crumbles around him.

The heroes struggle and suffer, wrestling with situations and decisions, finding courage to defy convention or speak their minds. The plays starkly juxtapose fate and free will. Oedipus was fated to kill his father and marry his mother. What difference could any of his actions make?

The plays ask spectators to consider moral dilemmas. Antigone decides whether to bury her dead brother, whom her uncle, the king, has declared a traitor, to be left for birds and dogs. She wrestles with divine law that says it is a woman's duty to bury the men in her family, and the man-made law of a tyrant. She chooses to bury him, and is sentenced to death. As a result, the king loses his son and

TRAGIC MASK: Actors changed masks to play multiple characters in one performance.

wife to suicide. The situations are intense, set in the long-ago Age of Heroes to allow perspective and distance.

There were two festivals in Athens, the rural and the city Dionysia. The rural festival, called the Lenaia, originally associated with agricultural fertility, began with a procession called the *pompe,* where our "pomp and circumstance" comes from. The women and men marched together, holding jars of water, jars of wine, woven baskets—and phalluses. Presumably these symbols of fertility were clay, although it's anybody's guess. Next were contests for dance troupes and choirs. Theater performances weren't added until 487 B.C.

The city Dionysia was an international festival, with six days of ceremonies, feasts, and back-to-back performances. During the time of the Athenian Empire, all member city-states sent representatives. As they entered the theater, each city was supposed to deliver a suit of armor and a bull for sacrifice. This display was one way Athenians lorded over the other Delian League members. There was another pompe, on a greater scale. The phallus carriers marched like the flag carriers at the opening ceremonies at the Olympics, as symbols of masculinity, fertility, and power. A team of people used a cart as a float, on which was an enormous phallus, too big to carry.

VASE PAINTING: This scene portrays a staged performance of Aeschylus's *Eumenides.*

The highlight of the festival was the competition among playwrights. The Theater of Dionysus in Athens had 17,000 seats, and was full to capacity. Women were not permitted to watch. Thespis won the first recorded competition in Athens in 534 B.C., and tradition gives him credit for introducing an actor in front of a chorus for the first drama—thus the word "thespian" for actor. Aeschylus, who lived from 525 to 455 B.C., introduced a second actor, allowing more action and dialogue. Sophocles, born about 30 years later, introduced a third actor. The ever-present chorus served as witnesses, commentators, and prophets.

Comedies were produced at the rural Lenaia festival of Dionysus. Playwrights set their comedies in contemporary times and resorted to physical comedy or scatological humor—mainly sexual innuendo and fart jokes. Aristophanes, who lived from about 450 to about 388 B.C., wrote satires that mocked powerful men for their vanity and foolishness.

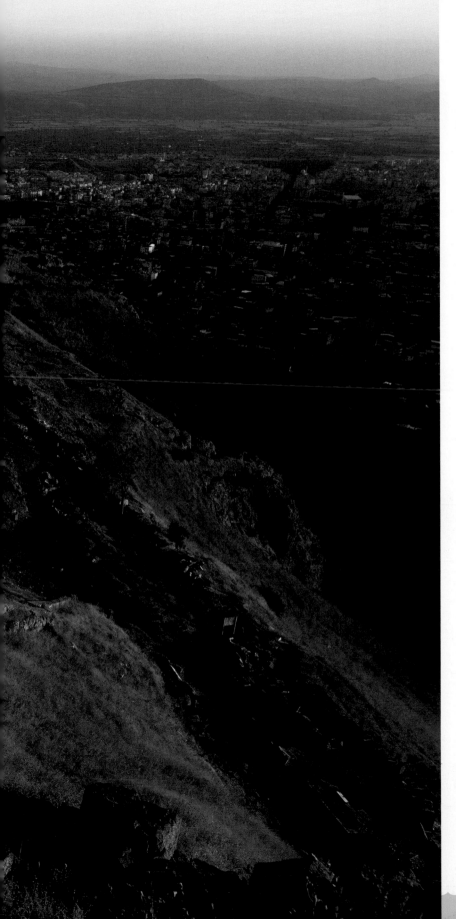

PERGAMON

❧

MOST GREEK CITY-STATES HAD theaters. Pergamon, or modern Bergama, near Miletus in Turkey, has a well-preserved theater that held 10,000 people. The steep slope afforded a marvelous view of the landscape, but the stage held people's attention. The 78 rows of seats are divided into three sections, built into the natural cliff of the acropolis. Pergamon has been continuously excavated since 1878 by the German Archaeological Institute.

Pergamon is best known for the sculptural decoration on the altar of Zeus. In the late 19th century, the Germans transported the altar of Zeus to Berlin. They reconstructed it along with other ancient structures in its own museum, a six-story building the size of a football field.

The Greek city-state of Pergamon is relatively young, established in the fourth century B.C., and was at the peak of its power in the third and second centuries B.C., when the theater was built.

STRONG WOMEN

CLYTEMNESTRA. Medea. Cassandra. Helen. Electra. Antigone. Iphigenia. These leading ladies were played by men in drag, in tragedies written by male playwrights, for a patriarchal society. Women were not even supposed to be in the audience. Out of hundreds of plays written and performed in the classical and Hellenistic periods, the complete texts of only 32 have survived to our day, and all of them except one include female characters. In so many of the tragedies, women defy male authority, challenge conventions, do what they want, and speak truth to power in ways that make the men seem weak, stubborn, blind, or just plain wrong. And yet these plays won awards granted by all-male judges. How?

Women were the voice of "the other": They were able to say things that the audience would be uncomfortable hearing from a man, or that were unorthodox or even dangerous to express in real life. However, the main reason these plays won is because they are just that good.

Audiences had strong reactions to these plays. Shortly after the Ionian Revolt that led to the Persian Wars, the playwright Phrynichus staged *The Capture of Miletus.* He experimented with setting the tragedy in his own time, rather than the Age of Heroes. That was a mistake. His play showed Miletus being taken back by the Persians after soldiers from Athens and Eretria fled, focusing on the fates of the freeborn Greek women of Miletus being taken by the victorious Persians as slaves. It was so heartbreaking that the Athenians passed a law saying no one could ever write another play set in contemporary times.

Euripides' tragedy *The Trojan Women,* produced in 415 B.C., explored the same theme, no doubt based on Athenian treatment of Melos the previous year, when the women of that conquered city also were enslaved. However, because he set the action in the Bronze Age, it was permitted, and it provoked the same emotional response. The mighty being brought low made for good theater. The turn of the wheel of fortune, one day free, the next a slave, was also a common plot for tragedy.

What gives a timeless quality to Greek tragedies is their complexity. There is never a clear hero or villain, male or female. We have empathy for both sides, and we watch them struggle. In Euripides' play *Medea,* the title character, a most unlikable woman who killed her children to spite her ex-husband, speaks powerful words that put her in a more

WINE CUP INTERIOR: A goddess carries to the altar a ritual bowl for making libations.

pitiful yet sympathetic light. Listen to Medea after learning that Jason has left her for a younger woman, and that the pair are engaged:

This thing undreamed of, sudden from on high, has sapped my soul: I dazzle where I stand, the cup of all life shattered in my hand, longing to die—O friends! He, even he, whom to know well was all the world to me, the man I loved, has proved most evil.—Oh, of all things upon earth that bleed and grow, an herb most bruised is woman. We must pay our store of gold, hoarded for that one day, to buy us some man's love; and lo, they bring a master of our flesh! There comes the sting of the whole shame. And then, 'tis they that face the call of war, while we sit sheltered, hid from all peril. False mocking! Sooner would I stand three times to face their battles, shield in hand, than bear one child.

Euripides captures the plight of women in ancient Greece, and helps the all-male audience see life from the female point of view. Of course, Medea proceeds to poison Jason's fiancée and kill her own children. It is, after all, tragic.

WOMAN AT ALTAR: An elegantly dressed woman attends to a tall incense burner.

ANOTHER KIND OF GREEK TRAGEDY

TERRIBLE DECISIONS AND A WAR of attrition left Greece in shambles after Sparta declared victory over the Athenian Empire in 404 B.C., the end of the Peloponnesian War. The allies freed from Athenian rule at first welcomed relief from tribute and oppression. But Spartans dealt with these other city-states in a heavy-handed way, installing their own troops inside cities, tearing down defensive walls, and overthrowing democratic constitutions.

Thebes rebelled in 379 B.C., led by the Sacred Band, their elite commando force composed of 150 pairs of male lovers. They overthrew Sparta's leadership over Greece at the Battle of Leuctra. The Thebans, bent on destroying Sparta, liberated the helots in Messenia, bringing down the Spartan economy. Sparta and Athens, among others, briefly joined to fight Thebes at the Battle of Mantinea in 362 B.C. Thebes won, but lost its general in the battle, and abandoned its rebellion.

What did the Thebans accomplish? Nothing, it seems. "War, which robs the ease of every day, is a harsh teacher," Thucydides wrote. Greek unity and harmony had been destroyed, and years of fighting weakened everyone. As the loss of life and waste of resources mounted, a new power was on the rise to the north, ready to take advantage of weakness: Macedonia.

PHILIP II

NORTH OF THESSALY and beyond the mountain pass of Thermopylae, Macedonia was on the fringe of the Greek world until the fourth century B.C. Its hereditary kings had reached out from time to time; around 500 B.C., one king tried to compete at the Olympics and was at first rejected for not being Greek enough. Only after he proved he was descended from Achilles could he enter a chariot race. The seminomadic Macedonian culture was more similar to the Balkans and the Russian steppes than to the Greeks—based on raising and riding horses, with no traditions of writing or literature, political theory, or higher education.

The experience of Philip II in Thebes changed all that. Philip, who lived from 382 to 336 B.C., spent a few years of his youth in Thebes, exchanged for a Theban prince to enforce a truce between Macedonia and Boeotia. Philip learned Greek warfare and tactics there, and received a Greek education. When it came time to educate his own son Alexander, he hired Aristotle to tutor him.

PHILIP II: This thumbnail-size ivory portrait was discovered in Philip's royal tomb, Vergina.

Philip became king in 359 B.C. For a few years, he raided nearby territories, conquering regions and absorbing them into Macedonia. He built a very large empire starting in northern Greece and then extending from Albania through the Republic of Macedonia to Bulgaria. His domain reached the Danube.

How did he keep these tribal, seminomadic people in line? He had been a hostage in Thebes to hold a truce. He used women to do the same. He married a daughter of the king in each area to seal allegiance.

Philip was a serious alcoholic who had male lovers, seven wives, and a taste for warfare. He had many children from all these wives, and there was always palace intrigue and rivalry.

Having unified northern Greece, Philip descended on central Greece, through the pass at Thermopylae, and then set his sights south. He seized two seats on the council that controlled Delphi. He interfered

LION HUNT MOSAIC, PELLA:
Alexander, right, and friend
Hephaestion, left, display courage.

in city-states allied with Athens. For 15 years he raided, harassed, destroyed, and interfered, unimpeded until Athens and Thebes united against him, unsuccessfully, at Chaeronea. The Athenian orator Demosthenes had been making speeches warning the Greeks to fight together against Philip, but too few had listened. Philip's victory in 338 B.C. made him the first king ever to rule over all the Greek city-states, unifying them for the very first time.

PHILIP'S TOMB

PHILIP II WAS KILLED in the theater at Aigai on the wedding day of one of his daughters. In one telling of the terrible story, one of his male lovers had become jealous of a new, younger one. The man complained to Attalus, Philip's adviser, who told him to come to a party that night. All would be smoothed over. At the party, Attalus arranged for some muleteers to sodomize the aggrieved man. Humiliated and seeking revenge, he intrigued to kill the king. Philip was buried in style, in a huge multichambered tomb filled with gold and silver, armor, and beautiful furniture. The tomb was found in 1979, partly looted in ancient times but still holding spectacular items, including a golden box that contained Philip's bones wrapped in a purple-and-gold shroud.

CREMATION BOX

PAYBACK: THE EXPEDITION TO PERSIA

MAP OF ALEXANDER THE GREAT'S ROUTE AND CONQUESTS: Note how small Greece is, in the upper left corner.

PHILIP IMPROVED HIS ARMY'S military equipment and tactics during his reign. Based on what he had learned in Thebes, he expanded the use of the cavalry, upping the numbers and having the horsemen gallop at just the right time from just the right angle to have maximum impact. By looking down on battles, Philip observed that the hoplite foot soldiers all equipped themselves with the same length of spear, marching in rows toward the center of the battlefield. What if he made the Macedonian spears a little longer? The opposing front line wouldn't get as close to the Macedonian front line, and the Macedonians could spear them first. He invented the *sarissa,* with a longer pike, revolutionizing hoplite warfare.

MAP KEY
- ■ Macedonia, 359 B.C.
- ■ Macedonia, 336 B.C.
- □ Empire of Alexander, 323 B.C.
- • City founded by Alexander
- × Major battle

ALEXANDER'S EXPEDITION INTO ASIA

April, 334 B.C.
Expedition begins

Alexandria founded in Egypt

Gaugamela

June, 323 B.C.
Death of Alexander

Granicus — Issus — Persian Gates — Aornos — Hydaspes

334 | 333 | 332 | 331 | 330 | 329 | 328 | 327 | 326 | 325 | 324 | 323

After beating the Greeks at the battle of Chaeronea, Philip assembled Greek representatives at Corinth, creating the Corinthian League. He tried to reassure them that they could keep their traditional constitutions and ways of life, although he required that they swear allegiance to him and his successors. To prevent uprisings, Philip needed to divert Greek attention toward a different common enemy, and the Persians came to mind. So he planned a campaign to lead the Greeks against the Persian Empire. He died before he could realize those grand plans.

The conquest of Persia was left to his son Alexander, who became king when Philip was assassinated, two years after the Battle of Chaeronea. He was 20 years old. Philip had treated him as a weak child in front of the Macedonian generals, so proving his legitimacy as king was difficult at first. To strengthen his claim, he buried his father like a Homeric king from the Age of Heroes, in the splendid tomb at Vergina.

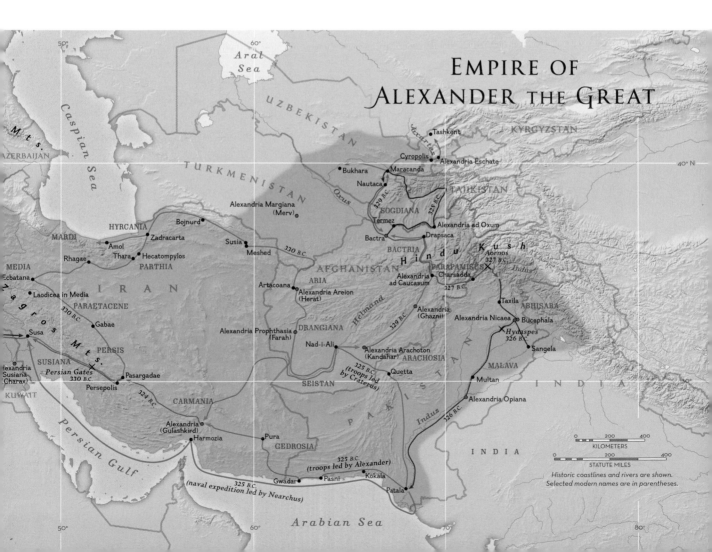

ALEXANDER THE GREAT

AS SOON AS ALEXANDER became king in 336 B.C., the northern territories that Philip had conquered immediately rebelled, taking Alexander away from the palace and up to Thrace. The Greek city-states weren't sure if they were liberated or not, following the death of Philip. Thebes revolted first, but within 48 hours Alexander and his army had marched 325 miles to quash the uprising. He killed all the men and enslaved the women and children. This was horrifying to the other Greeks, but it worked. No others rebelled.

Alexander would carry out his father's vision and surpass his achievements. Assembling a dream team of Macedonian generals, he recruited 30,000 troops and 6,000 cavalry from Macedonia and Greece to "liberate" the Persian subjects from their king. The excuse for the war was the sack of Greece by the Persians in 479 B.C., some 145 years earlier. It was a weak reason, but it inspired the Greeks. Alexander set out in 334 B.C. to retrace the footsteps of the Persian army. He would never return to Macedonia.

His fleet hugged the Aegean shore, docking to join the foot soldiers in the evenings, until they reached the Dardanelles. This narrow waterway leads from the Aegean to the Sea of Marmara through the Bosporus to the Black Sea. The European side had been home to Greek settlements for 300 years. Crossing the Dardanelles put Alexander's forces in Persian territory.

At this point, Alexander ought to have been preparing his troops for an offensive. He and a group of friends instead took the weekend off to sightsee at Troy. (Alexander slept with Aristotle's copy of *The Iliad.*) This is the first example of his many strange digressions and puzzling choices from a military perspective. The detour, although odd, did not hurt the mission.

ALEXANDER AND HIS HORSE:
Once tamed, Bucephalus went all the way to India with Alexander. Italian sculpture, 1530.

The army reunited and marched south to face their first battle at a geographically significant place, the Granicus River. Because the Persians underestimated Alexander, they didn't send enough men, and the Macedonians outnumbered the defenders. Eight Persian commanders were killed, and the leaderless troops ran. Alexander himself nearly died there, too, but was saved by his friend Black Cleitus, who chopped the arm off the man who was about to kill the king. The Persian emperor, Darius III, didn't even bother to show up, but he would join later battles.

After Granicus, Alexander declared himself ruler of the whole coast of Asia Minor. In spring of 333 B.C., the army continued south. Darius had been amassing an army of conscripts, more than 100,000, and had marched them from Iran to Turkey. Darius brought along his mother, wife, and daughters to watch the show. The armies fought at Issus, on the Turkish side of the border between Turkey and Syria. This one-hour battle changed history. Darius saw it turning out badly, and fled. A famous mosaic from Pompeii depicts this moment.

Alexander claimed the whole Persian Empire. He took Darius's women as hostages, but treated them well, posing with them to give himself legitimacy among locals. Darius wrote pitiful letters, bartering everything west of the Euphrates in exchange for his family. Alexander refused.

TIMOCLEA BEFORE ALEXANDER: Pardoned for killing her rapist, one of Alexander's soldiers

ALCOHOL IN MACEDONIAN SOCIETY

THE GREEKS DILUTED their wine, and most drank in moderation. Macedonians drank to get drunk, sometimes even before a meal was served. They had drinking contests, sometimes to the death from alcohol poisoning. They believed a treaty wasn't valid unless both signers were drunk. Holding one's liquor was a sign of masculinity, so it would need to be tested over and over. Philip was a mean drunk, verbally abusing his wives and children. Alexander abstained in his youth or drank very little. As his responsibilities increased, he found himself unable to resist the wine served at nightly parties, and he became a follower of the cult of Dionysus. While under the influence, Alexander killed his friend Black Cleitus, burned down the palace at Persepolis, and made other bad choices. Alcoholism tends to run in families, and looking back, we have little doubt that the men in the Macedonian royal family were alcoholics.

Before the Macedonians and Persians met again for their definitive battle, Alexander took the whole Mediterranean coast, including Syria, Lebanon, Israel, Gaza, and Egypt, where he was crowned a pharaoh and proclaimed a god. In 331 B.C. the Macedonians marched inland to face Darius at Gaugamela, close to Mosul in Iraq. Greatly outnumbered, the Macedonians still won.

Darius ran again, and this time Alexander pursued. Darius's own bodyguards murdered him. Alexander gave his enemy a royal burial.

Alexander took over the splendid Persian palaces at Persepolis, Pasargadae, and Babylon. He founded seven cities in Afghanistan, including Bagram and Kandahar. (The name derives from *Iskendar*, the Persian word for "Alexander.") Passing over the Hindu Kush, he fought the Punjabi King Porus in what is now Pakistan. To pacify the area of Tajikistan and Uzbekistan, Alexander married a Bactrian princess, Roxana. He staged a mass marriage between Macedonian soldiers and Persian women. He may even have sought to create an idealistic "brotherhood of man" based on merit, not ethnicity. This was all cut terribly short; when he fell ill and died at age 33 in 323 B.C. in Babylon, the ancient world had been transformed.

THE ALEXANDER MOSAIC, DETAIL: *(opposite)* Alexander defeating Darius in Battle of Issus, from Pompeii, House of the Faun

ALEXANDER THE BRAVE — OR JUST CRAZY?

ALEXANDER THE GREAT was a brilliant strategist with outstanding instincts. He could read a battlefield the way a world-class golfer reads a green. He was sensitive to local customs when he had to be, but took a stand when he needed to show strength. He had a great sense for theatrical tricks and stagecraft; he could make enemies think his troops were stronger than they were, or sway an audience with a gesture. With a few elite cavalry, he could appear days before the enemy expected him. He could motivate his troops to go to the ends of the earth. His men loved him.

But Alexander also cried a lot. There were days when he couldn't get out of bed or leave his tent. He was suicidal at least twice. He put himself in harm's way too eagerly at times. His choices appeared driven by megalomania. Sometimes he seemed possessed, with visions of himself rivaling Dionysus or Hercules, or believing his father was Zeus, not Philip. He veered off course to visit places on a whim, even when it endangered his men. He believed he was destined to unify "all mankind" by conquest.

Alcoholism? Bipolar disorder? Many diagnoses have been suggested, but historians have not agreed on why he acted as he did.

THE DEATH OF ALEXANDER THE GREAT in 323 B.C. signaled the end of the classical period, when Greece grew to glory. The new age, called the Hellenistic period, is all about fusion—of cultures, artistic styles, politics, and intellectual traditions. A touch of the Greek permeated all.

Alexander's veterans' colonies have had the most lasting influence. The old Greek colonies already extended as far north and west as Cadiz and Marseille. Now the Greeks also were far to the east, in Persepolis and Babylon. No matter who controlled these areas in coming centuries, their Greek character never fully disappeared. Retiring veterans and injured soldiers for whom the trip home to Macedonia or Greece was just too far, too dangerous, or physically impossible, were settled in at least 20 and possibly as many as 70 colonies. The colonists instituted Greek schools, law courts, and religious cults; they intermarried with local people. DNA tests on populations in Pakistan confirm that Europeans settled there 2,300 years ago. These cities include Kandahar in Afghanistan, and Samarkand in Uzbekistan, which became one of the most important outposts on the Silk Road, the trading route from Asia to Europe. But the city that has surpassed them all still bears its founder's name: Alexandria, Egypt, Alexander's gift to the future.

This Egyptian port remains the most important in the Eastern Mediterranean. The city itself was settled with soldiers too old to keep campaigning, and Jews from Jerusalem, who volunteered to move there. The Jewish quarter has been continuously occupied ever since. The 450-foot-tall lighthouse (called the Pharos) was one of the Seven Wonders of the Ancient World; built on a tiny island just off shore, the Pharos was an inspiration for the Statue of Liberty's flame. A large mirror kept the lighthouse working until an earthquake in A.D. 1323 toppled it. The Library of Alexandria was the center of intellectual life in the Hellenistic and Roman periods, holding scrolls of all Greek literature and thought, joined by Latin works once the Romans started writing anything worth reading. In A.D. 642, shortly after the founding of Islam, a Muslim army captured Alexandria, and their leader said, "If those books are in agreement with the Koran, we have no need of them; and if these are opposed to the Koran, destroy them." It took six months to burn them all.

Alexander also changed the eastern parts of the former Persian Empire. In Pakistan, his soldiers met a fierce army, complete with battle elephants. After Alexander defeated their King Porus, he ceded back the territory because he had found him such an able adversary. The next generation marked the beginning of the great Mauryan dynasty in India. It is said that as a boy, Chandragupta, founder of that empire, met Alexander in person.

In 323 B.C., the army reached Babylon, where, without warning, Alexander got sick and died. He had not named a successor, nor built a communications infrastructure to keep the vast empire together. Barely two years later, his power-hungry top men had partitioned his unified empire into 21 parts, but Greek remained the common language and Hellenism flourished.

DELPHI: The oracle and Temple of Apollo in the mountains of Parnassus

When the Romans took over Greece in 168 B.C., then all of Alexander's empire by 32 B.C., Greek rather than Latin remained the official language in those parts. When the Roman Empire split in two in the fourth century A.D., the eastern part had its capital in the old Greek colony Byzantium, founded in 657 B.C., rechristened Constantinople, now called Istanbul. Rome and the West fell to the Visigoths in A.D. 410, while Constantinople and the East carried on just fine. The Eastern Roman Empire continued as the Byzantine Empire, Christian but Greek Orthodox, until the Crusaders defeated it in A.D. 1204. By that point Byzantium was 1,860 years old.

From the "spooning" couple found in the Alopetra cave to the artifacts emerging from Thessaloniki's subway, new archaeological discoveries are enhancing, confirming, and challenging our understanding of the ancient Greeks. Scientific studies and techniques are informing us about the vapors that inspired the oracle at Delphi, and the pigments on the statue of Phrasikleia. Through the excavations of the lower town of Troy and the discovery of the Linear B tablet at Iklaina, we are learning about daily life outside the Bronze Age palaces.

From the theater at Pergamon to the temple at Delphi, natural landscapes and man-made architecture worked together to enhance the sense of awe and wonder and thus bring humans to spiritual and emotional heights. Plato and Aristotle, masters of reason and critical thinking, also believed that awe and wonder were the source of all wisdom. Greek poetry and drama exposed human flaws and inspired humans to avoid arrogance, abide by justice's laws, respect the gods and their powers, and treat all people as gods in disguise.

Learning about the Greeks can show us the big difference that individuals can make, and that should be inspiring. A simple case of laryngitis might have changed history—the speeches of Miltiades, Themistocles, Pericles, Demosthenes, and Alexander made all the difference in Greek history, which had a lasting effect on Western civilization.

There is hardly a facet of modern life that has not been touched by the ancient Greeks. Writers, artists, and philosophers explored the concepts of beauty and truth. Their love of the beautiful and their wildly imaginative myths and legends permeate Western arts and letters. One possible source of their creativity was their social networks. They had frequent opportunities to mingle with others and so generate and share ideas. Festivals, symposia, assemblies, and military campaigns were all settings for men to take part in rich conversations that led to new solutions, inventions, and discoveries.

The issues we face today are just as grave as those the ancient Greeks faced. We need the insights of Athena, the foresight of Apollo, the strength of Hercules, the justice of Themis, and the confidence of Zeus to solve them. We need the logic of Aristotle, the pursuit of truth of Plato, and the conscience of Socrates. We need their idealism.

For all their faults, the Greeks were open to new ideas and had a genius for cultural borrowing. They had a passion for dialogue and debate, and wrote masterpieces that resonate. They were willing to permit bold experimentation in their political life. They sought beauty in nature and in their art and architecture. They valued education, and were committed to the relentless pursuit of *arête,* excellence. The Greeks faced life with humor and joy, pursuing happiness through friendships, aesthetic experiences, and self-improvement. Let them be remembered and reinterpreted in every age and generation.

ACKNOWLEDGMENTS

THIS BOOK IS A LABOR OF LOVE, written for viewers like you of the PBS special, *The Greeks,* and visitors to the museum exhibition, "The Greeks: Agamemnon to Alexander the Great." I also had in mind travelers preparing to visit Greece, or readers who are interested in learning about ancient Greece for the first time, or after a very long time.

In this book, we looked at the high points of Greek civilization, and admittedly ignored the dark underbelly—slavery, poverty, imperialism, misogyny, and the miserable lives of the "great unwashed" or hoi polloi, as the Greeks would say. This book focused on the peculiar circumstances that allowed some Greeks to achieve great things and invent ideas that still shape the way we live today—the features of the Greeks that attracted me to study them in the first place.

It has been 40 years since I first went to Greece, and for me, the continuity between the ancient past and present makes the modern country a vibrant and exciting place to visit. I have had the opportunity to live in Greece, to give tours to alumni groups and the Smithsonian Associates, and to take students there. I see the Greeks more three-dimensionally because of my terrific students.

First, I wish to thank my editorial and creative team at National Geographic for their encouragement, trust, and most important, help. I also want to acknowledge the support of the Department of History, the dean of arts and sciences, and the Office of the Provost of The George Washington University, and especially the vice provost for faculty affairs, C. Dianne Martin. This work was supported by a grant from the GW University Facilitating Fund.

To my academic colleagues in classics, this book isn't written for you. It's for your parents, friends, and children, to help them understand what has kept a hold on you all these years. I hope this book will inspire more young people to take your courses in classical studies.

I dedicate this book to my supportive family: Eric, Hannah, Joshua, Max, Sandra, Bob, Elizabeth, Elaine, Janet, David, and Martin; and to my friends, who have been to Greece with me: Kimberly, Lisa, and Rebecca.

FURTHER READING

Beard, Mary. *The Parthenon.* Cambridge, Mass.: Harvard University Press, 2002, 2010.

Belozerskaya, Marina, and Kenneth Lapatin. *Ancient Greece: Art, Architecture, and History.* Los Angeles: J. Paul Getty Museum, 2004.

Broad, William J. *The Oracle: Ancient Delphi and the Science Behind Its Lost Secrets.* New York: Penguin, 2006.

Burkert, Walter. *Greek Religion.* Cambridge, Mass.: Harvard University Press, 1985.

Camp, John M. *The Archaeology of Athens.* New Haven, Conn.: Yale University Press, 2001.

Camp, John M., and Elizabeth Fisher. *Exploring the World of the Ancient Greeks.* London: Thames and Hudson, 2002.

Cartledge, Paul. *The Spartans: The World of the Warrior-Heroes of Ancient Greece, From Utopia to Crisis and Collapse.* Woodstock, N.Y.: Overlook Press, 2003.

Cline, Eric H. *1177 B.C.: The Year Civilization Collapsed.* Princeton, N.J.: Princeton University Press, 2014.

Cline, Eric H. *The Trojan War: A Very Short Introduction.* New York: Oxford University Press, 2013.

Etienne, Roland, and Francoise Etienne. *The Search for Ancient Greece.* New York: Harry N. Abrams Publishers, 1992.

Freely, John. *The Flame of Miletus: The Birth of Science in Ancient Greece (and How It Changed the World).* London: I.B. Tauris, 2012.

Garrison, Daniel H. *Sexual Culture in Ancient Greece.* Norman: University of Oklahoma Press, 2000.

Graves, Robert. *The Greek Myths.* New York: Penguin Classics, 1955.

Hale, John R. *Lords of the Sea: The Epic Story of the Athenian Navy and the Birth of Democracy.* New York: Viking, 2009.

Hall, Edith. *Greek Tragedy: Suffering Under the Sun.* Oxford: Oxford University Press, 2010.

Hall, Edith. *Introducing the Ancient Greeks: From Bronze Age Seafarers to Navigators of the Western Mind.* New York: W. W. Norton, 2014.

Hansen, Victor Davis. *The Western Way of War: Infantry Battle in Classical Greece.* Berkeley: University of California Press, 2009.

Harris, Diane. *The Treasures of the Parthenon and Erechtheion.* Oxford: Oxford University Press, 1995.

Hurwit, Jeffrey M. *The Athenian Acropolis: History, Mythology, and Archaeology From the Neolithic Era to the Present.* Cambridge: Cambridge University Press, 2000.

Kennell, Nigel. *Spartans: A New History.* Chichester, U.K.: Wiley-Blackwell, 2010.

Konstan, David. *Beauty: The Fortunes of an Ancient Greek Idea.* New York: Oxford University Press, 2014.

Lane, Melissa. *The Birth of Politics: Eight Greek and Roman Political Ideas and Why They Matter.* Princeton, N.J.: Princeton University Press, 2014.

Lefkowitz, Mary R. *Women in Greek Myth,* 2nd ed. Baltimore: Johns Hopkins Press, 2007.

Miller, Stephen G. *Ancient Greek Athletics.* New Haven, Conn.: Yale University Press, 2004.

Neils, Jenifer. *Women in the Ancient World.* Los Angeles: J. Paul Getty Museum, 2011.

Osborne, Robin. *Greek History: The Basics.* London: Routledge, 2014.

Powell, Barry. *A Short Introduction to Classical Myth.* Upper Saddle River, N.J.: Prentice Hall, 2002.

Sidebottom, Harry. *Ancient Warfare: A Very Short Introduction.* Oxford: Oxford University Press, 2004.

Spivey, Nigel. *Greek Sculpture.* Cambridge: Cambridge University Press, 2013.

Vandenberg, Philipp. *Mysteries of the Oracles: The Last Secrets of Antiquity.* London: Tauris Parke Paperbacks, 2007.

Wood, Michael. *In the Footsteps of Alexander the Great: A Journey From Greece to Asia.* Berkeley: University of California Press, 2001.

WEBSITES

Ancient Greek Religion: www.greekreligion.org

Ancient History Encyclopedia: www.ancient.eu

Athenian Agora Excavations: www.agathe.gr

Demos: Classical Athenian Democracy: www.stoa.org/projects/demos/home

Diotima: Materials for the Study of Women and Gender in the Ancient World: www.stoa.org/diotima

Internet Ancient History Sourcebook: legacy.fordham.edu/Halsall/ancient/asbook07.asp

Internet Classics Archive: classics.mit.edu

Internet Sacred Text Archive: www.sacred-texts.com

Perseus Digital Library: www.perseus.tufts.edu

POLIS by Stanford University: polis.stanford.edu

Theoi Greek Mythology: www.theoi.com

ILLUSTRATIONS CREDITS

(Cover), Oak wreath, possibly from Attiki, Late Hellenistic to early Roman period (gold sheet with repousse, chased & filigree decoration), Greek/Benaki Museum, Athens, Greece/Bridgeman Images; (back cover), Doug Pearson/JAI/Corbis; (spine), De Agostini/G. Dagli Orti/The Granger Collection, NYC—All rights reserved; (back flap), Courtesy of Diane Harris Cline; 1, Rare ancient Greek coin, Gold Stater, Macedonia, Alexander the Great 336 B.C. (photo)/Hoberman/UIG/Bridgeman Images; 2, Wolfgang Kaehler/Corbis; 4-5, CSP_sborisov/age fotostock; 6, PStelian Porojnicu/Alamy; 10, Cup, depicting a domestic bull, found in the royal tomb of Vaphio, Sparta, late Minoan I, ca 1500 B.C. (gold) (see also 148825), Minoan/National Archaeological Museum, Athens, Greece/Bridgeman Images; 12, HIP/Art Resource, NY; 13, Michael Schmeling/imageBROKER/Corbis; 15, Gianni Dagli Orti/The Art Archive at Art Resource, NY; 16, akg-images; 17, Tuul and Bruno Morandi/Getty Images; 18 (UP), RMN-Grand Palais/Art Resource, NY; 18 (LO), Bill Heinsohn/Alamy; 19 (UP), Gianni Dagli Orti/The Art Archive at Art Resource, NY; 19 (LO), John Hios/akg-images; 20, DEA/G. Dagli Orti/Getty Images; 21 (UP), Hulton-Deutsch Collection/Corbis; 21 (LO), Ashmolean Museum, University of Oxford; 22 (UP), Vanni Archive/Corbis; 22 (LO), Reconstruction of Knossos Palace, Crete, 20th century B.C. (color litho) Italian School/Private Collection/De Agostini Picture Library/Bridgeman Images; 23, Christian Heeb/JAI/Corbis; 24, Reconstruction of fresco of Procession, found in Palace of Knossos, detail: young men carrying offerings to goddess/De Agostini Picture Library/G. Dagli Orti/Bridgeman Images; 25 (UP), Melvyn Longhurst/Corbis; 25 (LO), HIP/Art Resource, NY; 26, HIP/Art Resource, NY; 27 (UP), Erich Lessing/Art Resource, NY; 27 (LO), Seal ring depicting a bull-leaping scene, late Minoan, ca 1500 BC (gold) (see also 419820), Minoan/Ashmolean Museum, University of Oxford, U.K./Bridgeman Images; 28-9, Gianni Dagli Orti/The Art Archive at Art Resource, NY; 30, Clay tablets with Linear A writing/De Agostini Picture Library/G. Nimatallah/Bridgeman Images; 31 (UP LE), DEA/G. Nimatallah/age fotostock; 31 (UP RT), DEA/G. Dagli Orti/age fotostock; 31 (CTR), Universal Images Group/Art Resource, NY; 31 (LO LE), DEA/G. Nimatallah/Getty Images; 31 (LO RT), Scala/Art Resource, NY;

32 (UP), Album/Art Resource, NY; 32 (LO), Replica of a snake goddess figurine, ca 1600 B.C., (glazed and painted earthenware), Minoan/Ashmolean Museum, University of Oxford, U.K./Bridgeman Images; 33 (UP), HIP/Art Resource, NY; 33 (LO), Michos Tzovaras/Art Resource, NY; 34, Lefteris Papaulakis/Shutterstock; 35 (UP), Gianni Dagli Orti/Corbis; 35 (LO), Vanni Archive/Art Resource, NY; 36-7, Zoonar/N Sorokin/age fotostock; 38, Lloyd K. Townsend, Jr./National Geographic Creative; 39 (UP), NASA/GSFC/METI/ERSDAC/JAROS, and U.S./Japan ASTER Science Team; 39 (LO), HIP/Art Resource, NY; 40, Reconstruction of ancient Mycenae (color litho), Italian School/Private Collection/De Agostini Picture Library/Bridgeman Images; 41, Funkystock/age fotostock; 42, Funkystock/age fotostock; 43, Vanni Archive/ Art Resource, NY; 44, World History Archive/Alamy Stock Photo; 45 (UP), Leemage/Getty Images; 45 (LO), RODKARV/Shutterstock; 46 (UP), DEA/G. Dagli Orti/Getty Images; 46 (LO), Dagger with gold inlays depicting an underwater landscape, from Routsi, Greece/De Agostini Picture Library/Bridgeman Images; 47, Leemage/Getty Images; 48, Gianni Dagli Orti/The Art Archive at Art Resource, NY; 49, Banet12/iStockphoto; 50, De Agostini/G. Dagli Orti/Getty Images; 51, De Agostini/A. Garozzo/Getty Images; 52, © The Metropolitan Museum of Art. Image source: Art Resource, NY; 53, Alvaro Leiva/Getty Images; 55, Bill Curtsinger/National Geographic Creative; 57 (UP LE), DEA/G. Dagli Orti/Getty Images; 57 (UP CTR), Gianni Dagli Orti/Corbis; 57 (UP RT), DEA/G. Dagli Orti/Getty Images; 57 (CTR LE), DEA Picture Library/Getty Images; 57 (CTR RT), DEA/G. Dagli Orti/Getty Images; 57 (LO), DEA Picture Library/Getty Images; 59, SuperStock/Getty Images; 60, DEA/G. Dagli Orti/Getty Images; 61, Heinrich Schliemann (1822-1890) German archaeologist. Excavations at Mycenae and Troy. Photograph 1877. Woodburytype/Universal History Archive/UIG/Bridgeman Images; 62-3, Yann Arthus-Bertrand/Corbis; 64 (UP), Iklaina Archaeological Project; 64 (LO), Iklaina Archaeological Project; 65 (UP), Brooklyn Public Library, Brooklyn Collection; 65 (LO), Express/Getty Images; 67, Pila, Palace of Nestor, reconstruction of throne room, watercolor painting/De Agostini Picture Library/G. Dagli Orti/Bridgeman Images; 68, The Trustees of the British

Museum/Art Resource, NY; 69 (UP), DEA/G. Dagli Orti/Getty Images; 69 (LO), North Carolina Museum of Art/Corbis; 70, Deutsches Archäogisches Institut—Athen; 71, Sergey Borisov/Alamy; 72, Gordon Gahan/National Geographic Creative; 73, Erich Lessing/Art Resource, NY; 74, Misja Smits/Buiten-beeld/Getty Images; 75, Sharon Mollerus/www.flickr.com/photos/clairity/3404411248/www.creativecommons.org/licenses/by/2.0/legalcode; 76, DEA/G. Dagli Orti/Getty Images; 78, Marco Simoni/age fotostock; 79, Gianni Dagli Orti/Corbis; 80, DEA/G. Dagli Orti/Getty Images; 81 (UP), Greece/Alamy; 81 (LO), DEA/G. Dagli Orti/Getty Images; 82, DEA /G. Nimatallah/Getty Images; 83, DEA/G. Dagli Orti/Getty Images; 84, Brian Seed/Getty Images; 85, René Mattes/age fotostock; 86, DEA/G. Dagli Orti/Getty Images; 87, Jon Arnold Images/DanitaDelimont.com; 90, bpk, Berlin/Staatliche Antikensammlung, Munich, Germany/Hermann Buresch/Art Resource, NY; 91 (UP), Martin Siepmann/Westend61/Corbis; 91 (LO), bpk, Berlin/Antikensammlung, Staatliche Museen, Berlin, Germany/Johannes Laurentius/Art Resource, NY; 92, The Metropolitan Museum of Art/Art Resource, NY; 93, Amphora with scene of Trojan War in relief, detail depicting Trojan horse, seventh century B.C./De Agostini Picture Library/G. Dagli Orti/Bridgeman Images; 94, Scala/Art Resource, NY; 95 (UP), DEA/G. Nimatallah/age fotostock; 95 (LO), Gianni Dagli Orti/The Art Archive at Art Resource, NY; 96, DEA/G. Nimatallah/age fotostock; 97 (UP), De Agostini Picture Library/Getty Images; 97 (LO), Leemage/Getty Images; 98-9, J. D. Dallet/age fotostock; 100 (UP), Araldo de Luca/Corbis; 100 (LO), The Trustees of the British Museum; 101 (UP), The Trustees of the British Museum; 101 (LO), The Trustees of the British Museum; 102, De Agostini Picture Library/Getty Images; 103, The Trustees of the British Museum; 104-105, The Trustees of the British Museum; 106 (UP), DEA Picture Library/Getty Images; 106 (LO), DEA/G. Dagli Orti/Getty Images; 107, DEA/G. Nimatallah/age fotostock; 108, De Agostini Picture Library/Getty Images; 109, DEA/G. Nimatallah/Getty Images; 110, The Trustees of the British Museum; 111 (UP LE), The Trustees of the British Museum; 111 (UP RT), The Trustees of the British Museum; 111 (CTR LE), The Trustees of the British Museum; 111 (CTR), The Trustees of the British

INDEX

Boldface indicates illustrations.

A

Achilles
  and Ajax **106**, 106–107
  and Amazons 105, 117
  in *The Odyssey* 59, 91
  and Patroclus 63, **161**
Acropolis, Athens **124, 140, 150, 168–169**
  building projects 166–167
  climbing 169
  plaques and statues **112, 117, 137, 179**
Adventure & exploration 80–89
  colonization 86–89
  Iron Age life **80**, 80–83
  rise of the polis 84–85
Aeschylus (playwright) 199
Aesthetics *see* Beauty, as ideal
Afterlife 186–187
Agamemnon, King (Mycenae) 44–45, 58–59
Age of Heroes 58–59, 75
Ajax **106**, 106–107
Akrotiri, Santorini 34–35, 39
Alcohol **146**, 209
Alexander the Great
  alcoholism 209
  and Amazons 105
  birth 177
  bravery **205**, 211
  colonization 212–213
  legitimacy as king 207
  map of empire 206–207
  oracles 191
  Persian conquest 133, 207, 208–209, **210**, 211
  in Troy 63
  tutored by Aristotle 159, **159**, 204
Alexandria, Egypt 212–213
Alphabet 83
Amazons **104–105**, 105, 117

Anacreon (poet) 172
Antigone 175, 185, 198–199
Aphrodite (goddess) 113, 114, **115,** 117, **117**
Apollo (god) 71, **116**, 116–117, 162, **173,** 190
Archaic period 7, 79, **87**
  map 88–89
Ares (god) 107, 113, **117**
Ariadne 27, **27**
Aristophanes 178, 194, 199
Aristotle
  Lyceum **158**, 158–159, **159**, 204
  philosophy 85, 109, 193
  on use of tribute money 141
Art 164–165
Artemis (goddess) 71, 116, **116**
Artemision, Cape 132–135
Asclepius (god) **162**, 162–163
Asia Minor
  Alexander's conquest 209
  coinage **111**
  Persian Wars 126–127
  philosophy 110, 156
Aspasia 178
Astronomy 171, **171**
Atalanta (goddess) **109**
Athena (goddess) **90, 113**, 114, 116
Athenian Empire 144, 145
Athens
  agora **84, 184**
  archaeological record 150
  athletes 100
  city-state 84–85
  civil unrest 102–103
  criminal justice **184**, 184–185
  democracy 125, 138–139, 152–153
  education 152–153
  monuments 79, **82**, 148
  Peloponnesian War 103, 151, 167, 183
  Persian War 128–130, 133, 136
  and Philip II 205

  plague 160
  political system 138–145, **139**
  Temple of Hephaestus **165**
  theater festivals 198–199
  Theseus as king of 102
  travel and trade 146
Athletics
  competitive spirit **100**, 100–101, **101, 107**
  discus throwers **94, 100**
  hygiene 101, **101**
  Olympic games **96**, 96–97, **97**, 100, **101**
Atlantis 37
Atom 109

B

Bacchanals 196, **196**
Bass, George 54
Baths 51, **51**
Beauty, as ideal 174–181
  gifts to the gods **174**, 174–175, **175**
  metalwork **180**, 180–181, **181**
  temples **176**, 176–177
  women's fashions 178, **179**
Beehive tombs **42**, 43, 51
Bisexuality 154, 164–165

C

Ceramics *see* Pottery
City-states, rise of 84–85
Cleisthenes **138**, 138–139, 153
Clocks 149, 185, **185**
Coinage 110, **111, 141**
Colonization 86–89, 110, 212–213
Competitive spirit 96–107
  Ajax **106**, 106–107
  Amazons **104–105**, 105
  animals **95**, 107
  athletics **100**, 100–101, **101, 107**
  Olympic games **96**, 96–97, **97**
  as value 90
  warfare **102**, 102–103, **103**

Computer, analog 171, **171**
Corinth 85, **87,** 89, 149, **162,** 163
Corinthian League 207
Corinthian order 177
Creativity 164–173
    Acropolis 166–169, **168–169**
    cultural 164–165
    inventions 170–171
    lyric poetry 172–173
Crete
    Mycenaean occupation 7, 40
    sacrifice 33, **33**
    and Santorini eruptions 38
    trade **57,** 74–75
    see also Minoans
Ctesibius (engineer) 170
Cultural events 192–197
Cycladic islands
    art **18,** 18–19, **19**
    earliest habitation 13
    island living 18–19
    trade 7, 15
Cyclops 137, **137**

D
Darius I, King (Persia) 126, 127, 130
Darius III, King (Persia) 208–209, **210,** 211
Daughter-cities 87
De Jong, Piet 25
Delian League 144, 145, **145,** 166, 183
Delphi **188–189,** 189
    Archaic cult statue **85**
    gifts to the gods 174, **174, 192**
    oracle 81, 86–87, 174, 190–191, **213**
    Panhellenic games 100, 189
Demeter (goddess) 68, 82, 112, 187, **187**
Democracy 125, 138–139, 152–153
Democritus (philosopher) 109
Didyma **190,** 191, **191**
Dionysus (god) **130,** 196, **197,** 198–199
Divorce laws 178, 184–185
Doric order 176
Drama **198,** 198–203, **199**
Drought 73–74, **74**

E
Earthquakes 38–39, 61, 74
Economic classes 141
Education 152–163
    ancient Greece 154
    Aristotle **158,** 158–159
    democracy needs 152–153
    health care 160, **162,** 162–163, **163**
    Plato 158–159
    Socrates **156,** 156–157
Egypt
    Persian control 144
    Sea Peoples 72–73
    trade with Greeks **52,** 52–53, **53,** 54, 56, **57,** 74–75
Eleusis **186,** 186–187
Elgin, Lord 41
Epirus 191
Euripides 196, 202–203
Evans, Arthur 20–22, **21,** 24–25, 27
Exploration *see* Adventure & exploration

F
Fashion 178, **179**
Fire 171
Fraternities 187
Frescoes
    Knossos **12, 17, 24,** 24–25, **25, 33, 53**
    Mycenae **48**
    Santorini **15, 34, 35,** 39
    technique 24
Frying pans 19, **19**
Funeral games 96
Future orientation 150–151

G
Gods *see* Religion
Gold wreaths 181, **181**
Grave markers 151

H
Hades 186–187
Health care 160–163, **162, 163**
Hellenistic period 212
Helots (slaves) 102, 118
Hephaestus (god) 113, 114, **165**
Hera (goddess) 112, 113, 116
Hercules 90, **90, 91,** 96, 102, 105, 113

Hermes (god) 173
Herodotus 105, 129, 135, 148
Heroes 90–95
    Age of Heroes 58–59, 75
    Greek values 90–91
    The Iliad and *The Odyssey* 92
    soldiers as 94–95
Heron (inventor) 170
Hesiod 81–82, 114, 117, 186
Hippocrates 160
Hippocratic oath 162, 163
Homer 96, 105
    see also The Iliad; The Odyssey
Hoplites (soldiers) 94–95, 118, **118, 120,** 120–121, **127,** 206
Hygieia (goddess) 162, **162**

I
The Iliad (Homer)
    description of Troy 60
    in education 153
    helmets 46
    heroes in 90, 92
    hospitality 87
    Trojan War 58
Infanticide 119
Intellectual curiosity 108–109
Inventions 170–171
Ionian Revolt 126–127
Ionic order 176–177
Iron Age
    adventure & exploration 80–83
    agriculture 80, **81**
    colonization 86–89
    introduction 7
    map 88–89
    religion 83
Island living 17, 18–19
Isthmia 100

K
Kalapodi **70,** 70–71
Knossos
    coinage **111**
    frescoes **12, 17, 24,** 24–25, **25, 33, 53**
    palace 20–22, **21, 22,** 24–25, **28–29,** 29
    storage rooms **72**

L

Law and order 182–191
  afterlife **186**, 186–187, **187**
  Athens **184**, 184–185
  Delphi **188–189**, 189, 190–191
  laws of all men 182–183
Leonidas (general) 133, **133**, 135
Leonidas (poet) 109
Linear A 21, 30, **30**, 35
Linear B 40, 64–67
  deciphering **64**, 64–65
  gods and goddesses 68–69
  Knossos 30, **32**, 66
  Pylos 66, **67**, 75, **75**
Lion Gate 41, **41**, 44
Lottery system **142**, 142–143
Love 154
Lyres 173, **173**
Lyric poetry **172**, 172–173

M

Macedonia
  alcohol 209
  expedition to Persia 206–207
  Philip II 103, **204**, 204–207
  wars 204–211
  see also Alexander the Great
Maps
  Alexander the Great's empire 206–207
  ancient Greek heartland 8–9
  modern Greece 13
  trade and colonization 88–89
Marathon, Battle of **128**, 128–129,
    148
Mariners, ancient 16–17
Matriarchy 32–33
Medical care 160–163, **162**, **163**
Medinet Habu Temple, Egypt 72–73, **73**
Melos 15, 16, 183
Metalwork **180**, 180–181, **181**
Miltiades (general) 128, 129
Minoans 20–33
  architecture **23**, 29
  engineering feats 50
  international trade 52–53
  Knossos frescoes **12**, **17**, **24**, 24–25,
    25, **33**, **53**
  mythology 26–27

palaces on Crete 7, 19, 20–22, **28–29**,
    29, 32
  pottery 30, 31, **31**
  sacrifice 33, **33**
  and Santorini eruptions 38
  women's roles 32
  writing system 21, 30, **30**
Minos, King 21, 22, 25, 26
Minotaur **26**, 26–27, **27**
Misogyny 82
Monuments 148–151
Mycenaeans 40–51
  beehive tombs **42**, 43, 51
  decline 70, 74, 75
  engineering feats **50**, 50–51, **51**
  food banks **48**, 48–49, **49**
  Mycenae palace **40**, 40–43, **41**
  occupation of Crete 7, 40
  Pylos palace 64, 66, **67**
  religion 68–69
  shaft graves **43**, 44–45, **45**
  trade 52, 53, 56, **57**, 74–75
  Trojan War 58–59, 60–61
  warriors 46, **46**, **47**
Mythology see Religion

N

Nemea 100
Nicocrates of Colonus 180
Nike (goddess) 95, **95**, **111**
Nudity 92, **92**, 164–165

O

The Odyssey (Homer)
  Cyclops 137, **137**
  in education 153
  heroes in 90, 92
  hospitality 87
  Nestor 83
  palace looting 74
  seafaring 14
  Sirens **91**
  Trojan War 58, 59, 61
  underworld 91, 106–107
Oedipus 81, 109, 119, 175, 198
Olympia 96–99, **97**, **98–99**, 155
Olympic games **96**, 96–97, **97**, 100,
    101

Orpheus 186
Ostraca **130**, 143, **143**

P

Paestum **108**, 194, **195**
Panacea (goddess) 162
Panhellenic games 100
Parthenon, Athens **144**, **166**
  construction 141, 166
  friezes **116**, **166**, **193**
  sculptures **102**, 174–175
  treasures 167, **167**
Peisistratus (tyrant) 102–103
Peloponnesian Wars 103, 183
  aftermath 103, 203
  cause 141, 183
  funding 167
  importance 150–151
  monuments 148, 149
Perfumes 49
Pergamon **200–201**, 201
Pericles **139**
  and Aspasia 178
  building program 141, 166–167
  death 160
  Delian League 144
  Funeral Oration 149, 150, 152
  public service 140, 142
Persephone (goddess) 68, 112, 187, **187**
Persia, Macedonian conquest of 206–
    211, **210**
Persian Wars 126–137
  Battle of Marathon **128**, 128–129
  Ionian Revolt 126–127
  monuments 148
  oracle at Didyma 191
  Persian warriors **126**, **127**, **136**
  Salamis 133, 136–137
  shipbuilding 130, **131**
  significance 103, 125
  Thermopylae **132**, 132–135, **134–135**
Phalanx 94, 120, **120**
Pheidippides (runner) 128, 129
Phidias (sculptor) 96, 166–167
Philip II, King (Macedonia) 103, **204**,
    204–207, 209
Philosophy 108–110, **110**, 156–158
Phrasikleia (maiden) 151, **151**

Phrynichus (playwright) 202
Pindar (poet) 97
Plato 37, 157, 158–159, 175, 194
Plutarch 121
Poetry **172,** 172–173
Polis 84–85
Poseidon (god) **4–5,** 61, **71, 111, 116**
Potnia (goddess) 32, 68–69, 71
Pottery 30, 31, **31,** 48–49, **49, 82**
Priam's Treasure 61
Prometheus 171
Pulak, Cemal 54
Pylos 51, **51,** 64, 66, **67,** 75, **75**
Pythagoras 109

R
Religion 68–71
    afterlife 186–187
    births of goddesses **113,** 114, **115**
    essence of gods 112–113
    gifts to the gods **174,** 174–175, **175**
    immoral immortals 116–117
    Iron Age 83
    Kalapodi **70,** 70–71
    Linear B tablets **68,** 68–69, **69**
    origins of universe 117
    roles of gods 116–117
    sacrifice 33, **33,** 69, **192**
    Theseus and the Minotaur **26,** 26–27,
        27

S
Sacrifice 33, **33,** 69, **192**
Salamis **111,** 133, 136–137, 148–149
Santorini 34–39, **36–37**
    Akrotiri 34–35
    as Atlantis 37
    colony 87
    earthquakes and volcanoes 34–35, **38,**
        38–39, **39**
    frescoes **15, 34, 35,** 39
Sappho (poet) 172–173, 175
Schliemann, Heinrich 44–45, 60–61, **61**
Sea Peoples 72–74, 75
Seafaring 14–19
Ships and shipwrecks 14–15, 54–55, **55,**
    130, **131**
Slaves 102, 118

Socrates **156,** 156–158, **157,** 178, 195
Soldiers 94–95, 118, **118, 120,** 120–
    121, **127,** 206
Sophocles 106, 175, 184, 185, 199
Sororities 187
Sounion, Cape **4–5, 71**
Sparta 118–121, **119, 133**
    archaeological record 150
    and Athenian Empire 144
    hoplite revolution 120–121
    infanticide 119
    military contests 102
    mothers and sons 121
    Peloponnesian War 103, 151, 183,
        203
    Persian War 127, 128, 132–133, 135
    Spartan way 118
Sponge diving 54
Symposia 193, 194–195, **195**
Syracuse 87, 89
Syria, trade with Greeks 53, 54

T
Temples, classical 70, 174–177, **176**
Thales of Miletus 109, 110
Theater **198,** 198–203, **199**
Thebes **52,** 56, **57,** 103, 136, 203, 204,
    205
Themis (goddess) 182, **182**
Themistocles 130, 133, 136
Thermopylae **132,** 132–135, **134–135**
Theseus **26,** 26–27, **27, 80,** 102, **103,**
    105
Thespis (playwright) 199
Thessaloniki 181
Thucydides (historian) 89, 145, 149,
    150–151, 160, 183, 203
Timekeeping 149, 185, **185**
Tiryns 50, **50**
Trade
    Bronze Age 15, 52, **52,** 74–75
    classical period 146, **147**
    luxury items 56, **57**
    map 88–89
Travel 146
Treasury of Atreus **42,** 43, 51
Tribute money 141, **141**
Trojan horse 59, **59,** 61, **93**

Trojan War 58–63, **59,** 106, **106**
Troy 58–63, **60, 62–63**
Tyrtaeus (poet) 132

U
Ulu Burun shipwreck 54–55, **55**

V
Values 82, 90–91
Vermeule, Emily 39
Volcanoes 34–35, **38,** 38–39, **39**

W
War and identity 204–211
Warfare laws 182–183
Weddings 82
Wine **146,** 209
Winged Victory of Samothrace **175**
Women
    athletics 100–101
    divorce laws 178, 184–185
    fashion 178, **179**
    health care 160
    in Minoan Crete 32
    misogyny 82
    Sparta 119
    in theater **202,** 202–203, **203**
Writing see Alphabet; Linear A; Linear B

X
Xenophon 156, 194
Xerxes, King (Persia) 130, 136

Z
Zakynthos **6**
Zeus (god)
    Athena's birth **113,** 114
    and Hermes 173
    law and order 182, **183**
    lovers 112, 114, 173
    oracles 191
    Prometheus and fire 171
    statue 97, **97**
    Temple **98–99,** 99

NATIONAL GEOGRAPHIC THE GREEKS:
    AN ILLUSTRATED HISTORY
Diane Harris Cline

PREPARED BY THE BOOK DIVISION

Hector Sierra, *Senior Vice President and General Manager*

Lisa Thomas, *Senior Vice President and Editorial Director*

Jonathan Halling, *Creative Director*

Marianne R. Koszorus, *Design Director*

R. Gary Colbert, *Production Director*

Jennifer A. Thornton, *Director of Managing Editorial*

Susan S. Blair, *Director of Photography*

Meredith C. Wilcox, *Director, Administration
    and Rights Clearance*

STAFF FOR THIS BOOK

Susan Straight, *Editor*

Maryann Haggerty, *Text Editor*

Moira Haney, *Senior Photo Editor*

Patrick Bagley, *Photo Assistant*

Kimberly Glyder, *Designer*

Debbie J. Gibbons, *Director of Intracompany
    and Custom Cartography*

Matthew W. Chwastyk, *Cartographer*

Marshall Kiker, *Associate Managing Editor*

Judith Klein, *Senior Production Editor*

Mike Horenstein, *Production Manager*

Rock Wheeler, *Rights Clearance Specialist*

Katie Olsen, *Design Production Specialist*

Nicole Miller, *Design Production Assistant*

George Bounelis, *Manager, Production Services*

Rahsaan Jackson, *Imaging*

Since 1888, the National Geographic Society has funded more than 12,000 research, exploration, and preservation projects around the world. National Geographic Partners distributes a portion of the funds it receives from your purchase to National Geographic Society to support programs including the conservation of animals and their habitats.

National Geographic Partners, LLC
1145 17th Street NW
Washington, DC 20036-4688 USA

Become a member of National Geographic and activate your benefits today at natgeo.com/jointoday.

For information about special discounts for bulk purchases, please contact National Geographic Books Special Sales: ngspecsales@ngs.org

For rights or permissions inquiries, please contact National Geographic Books Subsidiary Rights: ngbookrights@ngs.org

ISBN: 978-1-4262-1670-1

Printed in the United States of America

16/QGT-RRDML/1